CIBOLO TEXAS

The Early Years

Judy Womack
Sandra Lee Cleary

Copyright © 2019
by JUDY WOMACK and SANDRA LEE CLEARY
All rights reserved. No part of this book may be used or reproduced in any manner whatsoever without the written permission of the author.

Womack, Judy and Sandra Lee Cleary
Cibolo Texas: The Early Years
ISBN 978-1-941516-45-4
First Edition
History

ISBN Paperback: 978-1-941516-45-4
ISBN eBook: 978-1-941516-46-1

Published by Franklin Scribes Publishers
Franklin Scribes is a registered trademark
of Franklin Scribes Publishers
franklinscribeswrites@gmail.com
franklinscribes.com

Contact the author at
franklinscribes.com/sandra-lee-cleary
facebook.com/Sandra-Lee-Cleary-505581149605790

Front and back covers by Thompson Printing Solutions
This book was printed in the United States of America.

Dedication

Cibolo's rich, colorful, and amazing history has been hidden for too long. What has already been told about the city and its surroundings begins in 1968 when the town was incorporated. However, we wanted to delve in and share more about Cibolo's early years. The early Indians and the people who brought their cultures with them made Cibolo what it is today. They deserve recognition, applause, and admiration for the hardships they faced to settle this beautiful area. We have gathered information from many sources and compiled it all here for those who live in Cibolo today and for the many generations to come. We hope you enjoy it.

Table of Contents

Crossroads 1

People of the Valley 15

Thomas Perryman 21

The Chisholm Trail...................................... 48

Forgotten Roads and Texas Travelers......... 49

Civil War 109

The Railroad 117

Post Office 120

Schools... 122

Economic Conditions 126

The Town of Cibolo 133

WWI in Cibolo and Schertz 146

Bank Robbery in New Braunfels 171

Entertainment 172

The Grange on Main Street 174

Newspaper Articles 216

Sources 220

Index... 227

CROSSROADS

It was a crossroads for Indian tribes.

It was part of a trail to follow from the Rio Grande to Louisiana.

It was grassland for enormous ranches.

It was the start for dreams and aspirations for those oppressed in their own country.

It was the place of beginning again.

It was . . . and is . . . Cibolo.

* * * *

Crossroads

Arrowheads and bits of Native American culture can still be found around the curving Cibolo Creek and in the Cibolo Valley. The Wichita, Karankawa, Caddo, Lipan, and Tonkawa Indians all liked the grassy banks and hidden spots and came to camp for several months in the summer on the springs. The bison, to the east and west of the valley, could be hunted on the black lands, and the Tonkawa tribe was known to be friendly. They also shared land with the Coahuiltecan tribes south of them in what is Bexar County today. All the Indian tribes lived in scattered villages of teepees. They ate fish and small game but not coyote or wolf because of religious taboos. Stories of cannibalism were told of the Tonkawa, but the other tribes they met were not afraid of them.

In the late 17th century, maps were needed to show the connection from central New Spain across the missions and presidios into Spanish Texas. There was a link from Mexico City to Mission San Juan Bautista on the south side of the Rio Grande, then on to San Antonio, what would become New Braunfels, then east to Nacogdoches, and Louisiana. It became known as El Camino Real de los Tejas, the King's Highway, and stretched 2500 miles.

For more than one hundred fifty years, this was the only route for overland travel from the Rio Grande. The ever-changing route, a rough network of cattle trail, military road, and immigrant passage, connected Texas to all parts of Mexico and Louisiana. Moses AUSTIN would have taken the trail when he went to San Antonio to discuss the Austin Colony with officials. His son Stephen F. AUSTIN would have done the same. Davy CROCKETT came into Texas as others before and followed the familiar route on his way to the Alamo. In some of the early diaries, the Cibolo Creek and even an Indian tribe called the Cibolo are noted. An example is careful writing on a journey in 1691 by Domingo Teran de los RIOS, first governor of Texas, in which he mentions camps of the Cibolo Indians.

Martìn de ALARCÒN, a knight of the order of Santiago, governor of Coahuila and Texas from 1716 to 1719, then later, founder of San Antonio, writes in his diary of camping at "Sibulo Creek." During his 1718 expedition, he mentions the live oaks, hackberries, and elms along the creek. In 1791 Josè de Azlor y Virto de VERA, governor of Mexican provinces of Coahuila and Texas between 1719 and 1722, writes of going to San Antonio de Behr and crossing the Cibolo Creek. This creek was described in later writings as a spring of flowing, cold water within a creek of warm, brackish water. The land between the Cibolo and Guadalupe Rivers was considered to be the best around for grazing and pasture land.

The name for the creek was an Indian word meaning bison. Some of the first spellings of the word varied: CIVVILLO or CIBBOLO. The creek was a clean stream with watercress growing along its banks. Some even reported catching shellfish in it. Indians told stories of stampeding bison across the steep banks so that the animals would land in the beds of the stream and be unable to stand, thereby making for an easy kill.

A ranch related to Mission San Antonio de Valero, more popularly known as the Alamo founded in 1718, was Rancho de Monte Galvan, a large acreage bound by Cibolo Creek. Missionaries taught Indian men to care for the livestock. These Indians, and sometimes their families, lived part of the year on the ranch. They became known as cowboys or vaqueros. Other missions also had ranchos associated with them to help supply their needs. Among them were the following: Rancho del Paistle, Rancho Leal, Los Corralitos, Rancho Gortavi, San Antonio del Cibolo, San Miguel de Amoladeras. By 1782, more than 1200 men, women, and children lived in or near the Presidio San Antonio de Bèxar, a Spanish fort built near the San Antonio River.

Spanish land grants gave numbers of

ranchers the chance to make money by developing herds and trading animals along the Cibolo Creek. By 1825 heads of families could apply for a league (4428.4 acres) for grazing and a labor (177.1 acres) for cropland. They had grand-sounding names like Rancho de San Francisco and Rancho de San Antonio del Cibolo, but it was just acres on paper that had to be organized and run by someone, and the distance from Mexico often proved too much for an owner to manage.

Still the maps showed the breakdown of the area into divisions, and those who had the money and wanted to try and prosper in the Cibolo Valley received land grants. The Cibolo Valley was often called "La Huerta del Mindo" or Garden of the World because the soil seemed good for farming and grazing. Between 1776 and 1836, maps were made for as many as twenty-six ranchos in the area around San Antonio.

As Texas fought for its independence from Mexico in 1836, Cibolo stayed in the heart of the dramatic action. According to some reports, Davy CROCKETT and some other officers rode out to Cibolo Creek Crossing in February of 1836 to wait for and escort volunteers to the Alamo, but none came. After the Alamo defenders fell, President General Antonio Lòpez de SANTA ANNA sent a division of 600 men toward Bastrop, expecting them to give aid against General Sam HOUSTON. This group of men plundered everything along the way but eventually lost their way in the pines near Bastrop and were unavailable to give help. It is possible that SANTA ANNA's forces marched through a lower part of the Valley after the Alamo on their way to defeat at the hands of Sam HOUSTON. With independence came the question of who would take up the spaces vacated by the Spanish owners. The answers changed the landscape of Cibolo forever.

In the fall of 1842, General SANTA ANNA, now president of Mexico, directed raids into Texas to cause as much mayhem as possible. This continued until the summer when more Mexican forces were sent including 1400 soldiers and 200 Indian scouts whose job was to march on San Antonio and take control. Texans, upon hearing of the assault, gathered under the command of Col. Matthew "Ole Paint" CALDWELL and made camp at Cibolo Creek. The clash between the two groups resulted in the Battle of Salado Creek with the Mexican group suffering heavy losses.

A bold plan took shape at the same time across the Atlantic Ocean that would have a profound effect on Cibolo. As the spring of 1842 began, twenty-one noblemen met in Germany to form a society known as the Mainzer Verein or Adelsverein. Their goal was to establish a new Germany in Texas by means of an organized large emigration. Poverty was oppressive in Germany, and young men had no place to work. By law, most farms could not be divided, and prices paid to farmers were low. Reports were that it was so bad in many places that no one could afford to buy sugar.

Two agents were sent to discuss the options with President Sam HOUSTON. After tough times of declining some land grants and accepting others, the Adelsverein acquired land north and west of San Antonio. In 1844 the group was formally constituted as the Society for the Protection of German Immigrants in Texas. Prince Carl of Solms-Braunfels was dispatched to be General Commissioner, and when he arrived, a series of negotiations and agreements fell apart over colonization contracts. No preparations were made for the people who would come after him. Nevertheless, the first immigrants arrived in Texas in December 1844 and early 1845. Carlshaven, the name they gave to the place where they came on land, was an open and undeveloped marshland with no buildings, tents, water, food, or supplies. Chosen because it was at the mouth of the Guadalupe River, it could be used as a guidepost to their new homes. By spring over 6,000 Germans had arrived. For shelter, they dug holes in the ground for poles, then laid branches and twigs on top covered with bed sheets or tablecloths. Teamsters who had been hired to transport them were contracted to go away. The rains made the area a swamp. Malaria, dysentery, cholera, yellow fever all made short work of the weakest of the people. An outbreak of spinal meningitis was also devastating.

Finally, the rains stopped, and those who were physically able started for the Valley on foot, leaving behind their household goods and sick relatives. They left a trail of death from Carlshaven to New Braunfels; no more than 1,500 of those who had come ashore made it to their new home. Only one in four survived. Those who were sick brought their diseases to the Cibolo, and in New Braunfels they were placed under a shed constructed of pilings with a reed roof. If they died, coffins were not made because boards were not available. Bodies would be wrapped in sheeting and carried out to the cemetery.

Fording the Guadalupe River was also difficult for some because they had never forded a river in Germany. The trip meant crossing the river in several spots before they arrived at their destination. Some people lost all their supplies in the waters or watched helplessly as family members drowned.

But the stories of this new place in Texas continued to lure German families so that another thousand followed the initial groups. The Adelsverein proved to be a failure in many ways. Finally, facing bankruptcy, they attempted to revive the society under a new name: German Emigration Company. Because the original nobles had no real business sense or understanding of what it would take to start a massive undertaking like this, it would be easy to take advantage of them. The German Emigration Company advertised that a married settler could receive 640 acres for a land grant and that the cost for setting up this achievement would be less than $2000. So, the Germans kept coming despite the hardships they were sure to face. A typical journey would be like one aboard the Neptune. The ship, 115 feet long and 27 feet wide, carried 214 passengers and 17 crew. It was not an easy undertaking for anyone. Weekly rations aboard ship for each adult amounted to four ounces of coffee, two ounces of tea, eight ounces of sugar, seventeen ounces of butter, three to five pounds of bread, and a quarter bottle of wine. For the entire voyage, each adult received drinking water and thirty pounds of potatoes.

Once on land, bands of Indians, mostly Comanche, came down on the unprotected causing even more problems and loss of life. A letter to the Governor in 1855 told the story of horses being stolen and even the death of a slave and a young boy, the son of a preacher near the stage crossing at Selma, that still stands there today.

Jouette MCGEE, second oldest child of Rev. MCGEE, the Methodist circuit rider, was taken and killed in July of that year. Most of the residents had gone to a barbecue near Seguin when Indians tried to take the young boy and a Negro girl. She was carrying water from Lipan Creek, screamed, resisted the attack, and was killed. The same thing happened to young McGee.

W.T. SCULL, a close friend of William

TRAVIS, left with Jim UMPHREYS, and Silas HARMON to follow the Indian attackers. Those left on the SCULL farm as well as relatives and slaves headed for Seguin but hid in a gully at first, a mile and a half from the SCULL farm. Later, they spent the night with a friendly neighbor and then returned home when the men returned. The letter to Austin states:

The Apache Lipans, led by Chief Duelgas de CASTRO, had signed an earlier treaty with the Texans and were no threat at all, but some of the other tribes were not happy with what was happening to their camping grounds. A clash with those coming in was bound to happen as the numbers of Germans as well as other settlers increased.

Land grant records for the area after Texas became a republic showed a number of names, some Anglo and some Spanish. They were:

RECTOR, Clairborn
MILLER, David
BAXTER, William Chester
LEAL, Jeronimo
GARCIA, Trinidad
DOMINGUEZ, Sexto
DE LA GARZA, Frailon
DE LOS SANTOS COY, Emanuela
CADENA, Jose Maria

GRAY, James
SAN MIGUEL, Pedro
RICHARDSON, James
LINDENBURG, Mathias
LEMON, William
THOMPSON, Hiram
BRACKEN, William

ABSTRACT OF TEXAS LAND OFFICE
LAND CLAIMS IN GUADALUPE COUNTY
1852

Alsbury, Y. P.	1,476 acres
Alsbury, Thomas	1,470 acres
Bradley, James	4,500 acres
Bizby, Horace	610 acres
Brown, Rufus	640 acres
Brown, Mary	640 acres
Bracken, William	320 acres
Bennett, Val	3,400 acres
Coy, Emile L. Santos	2,502 acres
Cardvajal, Franco	4,300 acres
Cadina, Jose Maria	320 acres
Chenauld, Felix	320 acres
Cockrell, Sam	320 acres
Davis, Dan	320 acres
Flores, Jose	4,600 acres
Garcia, Trinidad	1,476 acres
Graves. Charles	649 acres
Guerra, Juan	313 acres
Green, Alanson	280 acres
Holderman, Jesse	320 acres
Highsmith, A.M.	320 acres
Jack, James	640 acres
Leal, Geronimo	2,952 acres
Lewis, A.S.	640 acres
Leman, William	640 acres
Mitcheli, Vicente	4,500 acres
Morgan, Joseph	1,476 acres
Miller, David	300 acres
Murphy, James	1,920 acres
Rector, Claiborne	4,426 acres
Rodriguez, Francisco	1,453 acres
Smith, Peter	640 acres
Scantleberry, W.	320 acres
Torres, Guadalupe	2.834 acres
Williams, Joshua	974 acres

Tennessee-born **RECTOR** was at the Battle of San Jacinto and received a land patent in 1840. He later was postmaster at La Vernia. Two years earlier in 1838 **BRACKEN** received land and in 1849 received more land from a grant from the governor. He was an original colonist who came with Green **DEWITT** to **DEWITT'S COLONY** and was also an intelligence gatherer and courier during the War against Mexico. It was because of his service he was eligible for land. He had also been in a survey group which came to the Cibolo area in 1835. This is when he decided to file for acres there. When he died in 1852, his will proved to be a legal argument for more than twenty years as he dictated that his three mulatto children were to be set free, educated, and share in his large estate. None of his wishes were carried out. His land on the Cibolo was carved from land which had originally belonged to Vicenti **MICHELI**'s league, the first Italian merchant to settle in Texas.

MICHELI arrived in Nacogdoches in 1793 and established his Rancho de San Francisco northeast of San Antonio. A number of the land owners received land from the Republic because they had arrived as single men. They lived there for three years, and then applied for at least 320 acres, and in some cases, 640 acres.

CADENA, LEAL, GRAY, DE LE GARZA and **LINDENBURG** were the subject of a lawsuit which reached the state Supreme Court in 1854 over their knowledge of a gambling table. However, Lindenburg made his way through that hurdle and later became a grocer.

THOMPSON was both a preacher and farmer and lived to an old age in another part of Texas. All the lands were surveyed by the state surveyor who used markings such as live oak trees, mounds of stones, hackberry trees, Cibolo Creek, or anything in nature that could be cited.

German language newspapers were established: *Neu-Braunfelser Zeitung*, *San Antonio Deusche Zeitung*, and *San Antonio Staats-Zeitung*. More newspapers started in other areas so that the new immigrants could know what was happening throughout their communities and the state in the language they knew.

Between 1850 and 1860 small communities sprang up all over the Valley. New Berlin, for example, was in the eastern part of the Valley and had a few educated residents: Friedrich VORDENBAUM, a trained minister, rode the circuit between Houston and San Antonio, often sleeping on the banks of the Brazos or Colorado until the rivers receded enough for him to cross.

Edward TEWES spoke several languages. Ferdinand DIETZ had a gold medal which had been presented to his father by Napoleon after he had been a guest of the Dietz family on a journey from Russia.

Others who came were a combination of

simple farmers and intellectuals, all willing to endure the hardships of this new place. They were predominantly Lutherans and Catholics. The Bishop of the Catholic Church in 1852 sent a letter to the Franciscans in Europe saying priests would be needed to celebrate mass in the areas of Santa Clara and Cibolo since it was beginning to grow.

Two of the early settlers returned to Germany for a visit and praised the "Smiling Valley of the Cibolo" so much that their friends grew tired of hearing of it. Fights resulted, and the visitors were arrested for breaking the peace.

Travelers continued to write about the area. One wrote in 1857 that when his party left New Braunfels, they crossed to Cibolo, pronounced by Texans as Sewilla, and reported that the Creek disappeared in its course sometimes, leaving the bed dry.

Roads were very important now that more people were arriving. In 1852 citizens petitioned to the county for a new road as a route to New Braunfels. Also, they asked for a road to be laid out from the Seguin courthouse on the best line to the Cibolo so as to establish a road to San Antonio. These would not be great highways but would mean clearing as much brush as possible to help wagons, carts, and horsemen get to a certain point.

At the grand jury in fall of 1859, Friedrich PFANNSTIEL was named a member, a sign that Valley residents were taking part in government.

PERRYMAN was given the title of presiding election officer for the elections. He was also appointed Captain of Patrols for the District which meant he and four others were to be prepared to answer when a call for help came from citizens or a dispute developed. And citizens were certainly more numerous now as the value of area farms increased by almost 600% by 1860, making newcomers more willing to endure the hardships.

People of the Valley

The area had a doctor – Dr. Felix BRACHT and later Dr. Hilmar JACOBSON. BRACHT resided near Cibolo Creek since 1849 after arriving with his brother Viktor on the brig Herschel. Viktor  wrote a very popular book called *Texas In the Year 1848* which had become a guide for the thousands of German immigrants who were pouring into the area. In the book, he advised new settlers to bring barrels of bacon, ham, our, crackers, sugar, dried apples, rice, beans, salt, pepper, and a cask of tea. The brothers were considered revolutionists in Germany and part of the Forty Eighters who left after elections threatened their independence. They were both well educated and interested in learning of all kinds. Dr. BRACHT taught at a private school in New Braunfels as well as practiced medicine. He purchased 400 acres and built a sturdy home with a large porch. When his daughter Felicitas BRACHT married Edward STAPPER, the two families had a very strong relationship, and the families lived under the same roof for many years on a place that would later be known as the STAPPER farm. People who needed medical attention came to the farm. Dr. BRACHT lived to an old age in San Antonio.

Dr. JACOBSEN taught school before he studied medicine with his office in the house he had built across from church property. His time was shortened, however, by his own unsuccessful appendectomy.

By 1860 an area called LOWER VALLEY had at least eighty families with fifty-six having a German surname. The post office, called VALLEY POST OFFICE, was on the stage stop going toward New Braunfels and Bastrop. Thomas J. PERRYMAN was designated as postmaster on July 2, 1861 and held the job for the next five years during the War.

Some of the names on the 1860 census for Lower Valley were:

PERRYMAN, Thomas
GIVENS, John
CONRAD, Carl
ANDERSON, W.W.
CONRAD, Herman
DABNEY, William
BROTZ, Dorothy
SCHRAUB, Sophia

SCHMITZ, August
STAMITZ, Lawrence
GERHARD, George
KNIBER, John
MEURIN, T.P.
DIETZ. Ferdinand
PFANSTIEL, Fred, J.P.
HOFFMANN, Henry.
OELKEN, Henry
SEILER, William
REINHOLD, James
ORR, Henry
RINEHART, Frank
SNIDER, Charles
HEGER, Charles
BERTIER. Charles
HEGER, Fred
BURBANK, James
HILD, George
JOHNSTON, W.B.
CRUEGER, Charles
YOUNG, John
LINN, Ernst
BERGFELT, J.G.
STAPPER, T.L.
YEHL, Fred
YEHL, William
SCHLATHER, Jacob
SCHLATHER, George
RITTIMANN, John

AMACHER, Melchior.
SUSSMANHAUSER, Ludwig
PFIEL, Anton, August, Edward, Jacob

By 1870 several African American families were farming in the VALLEY. They included:

FIELDS, Henry, Isaac
SMITH, Milton
HENDERSON, George
THOMAS, Eliott
SHEPHERD, Jack
SMIDLEY, John
HIGGINS, Joseph
TAYLOR, Jack
PRESTON, Prekill
ROBINSON, James
ANTHONY, Abraham
JACKSON, George
LATIMER, Ben
GRIFFIN, Alfred
THOMAS, Kilfer
TORRY, Julian
SNEED, Harrison
FORTUNE, Francis
GRAVES, Moses

The lone family of Mexican heritage was that of Jesus GARCIA who, with wife Susan and three children, had been in the Valley long enough to be counted on the census.

Three years before this in 1867, Jacob SCHLATHER, son of William SCHLATHER, had bought land in the VALLEY. He and his family came to America aboard the *Anna Elise* in 1852, settled in New Braunfels, and became a naturalized citizen in 1858. He planned to concentrate on farming, but he then sold the land to his brother George SCHLATHER who decided to open a general store because there were enough residents who needed a place to buy goods and were tired of making a long trip to other locations.

He was joined in the store by Ernst JENULL who knew something about the grocery business after clerking in San Antonio at a number of grocery establishments. He had received his naturalization papers in 1863. JENULL also became the postmaster at the store before he bought land and later turned his attention to ranching.

The store held a variety of things for the people of the VALLEY who came to shop. Some items for sale might have been: plugs of chewing tobacco from a larger block, horse collars, lamp chimneys, shoes, salt, plow points, rope, coffee, sugar, lard, patient medicine, fabric, crackers, crockery, and clothing. One yard of calico was seven cents; one spool of thread – five cents; a bar of soap – five cents. Items that sold well would be re-ordered, and those that didn't would be pushed to the back.

One of the first buildings in the Valley

besides the store was St. Paul's Church. George SCHLATHER donated a triangular piece of land to the Evangelical Reform Church. In 1876 a small wooden church was built on that property, and the first pastor, Rev. Oscar SAMUEL, who had been a teacher, drafted a constitution for the congregation, which was signed by nineteen members.

Johan George BERGFELD operated a dry goods store. Only in his twenties, BERGFELD had received his naturalization papers in 1858 shortly after he arrived in Texas. His marriage to Gertrude STAPPER made him part of one of the more solid families in the county.

Gottfried WELLER and his wife Anna Schlather WELLER had come by way of Galveston in 1867. WELLER brought his ability as a brickmaker, a trade he taught his son. The area was growing with each day, but a dramatic event was about to take place.

THOMAS J. PERRYMAN

THE RICHEST MAN IN THE VALLEY
GUADALUPE COUNTY, TEXAS

1809-1877

The Perryman family had been in America before the American Revolution and Georgia became home to many family members, with comforts and a solid reputation.

The first PERRYMANS were in Bristol, England in the 1600s but joined the waves of immigrants to the Colonies in the years that followed the first successes for sustainable life. Richard PERRYMAN, born in Halifax, Virginia in 1722, married Martha DEJARNETTE; her birth name would come to be used by later family members as a first name.

Their son, Harmon PERRYMAN, born in Warren, Georgia, Wilkes County in 1760, fought as a young man in the Battle of King's Mountain under Captain ROBERT SEVIER. When SEVIER was wounded, and his troops told to retreat, he refused to leave his position on the field. Later, HARMON and two others carried SEVIER to receive treatment. Sadly, his wounds proved fatal, and SEVIER died nine days later with his name ever connected to bravery and honor on the field of battle.

After the war in 1785, Harmon married Margaret VINING. They began buying land in Georgia and Alabama. He realized there was money to be made this way and took chances with unpopulated plots of land that he bartered in exchange for other pieces. For his efforts in 1813 and 1815, he became Justice of Interior Court for Twiggs County. He was involved in the 1807 and 1827 Land Lotteries. He owned at least twenty-one slaves to work his 1250 acres in Twiggs County and 940 acres in Jones County. Buying and trading land gave him a reputation as someone not afraid to take a gamble where land was concerned.

Thomas PERRYMAN was born in 1809 to a family who by now had accumulated wealth and status in the community. The youngest of nine children, seven boys and two girls, Thomas had the luxury of attending the University of Georgia in Athens on the banks of the Oconee River. However, Thomas did not seem to excel in the classroom or even to remain on campus to finish a degree. He returned home. Thomas may have been married

1830 to 1832 although there is no record of it. However, records show two sons born to him during this time, Harmon AUGUSTUS or H.A. named for Thomas' father, and James. Thomas would have been a young man of twenty-one or twenty-two. His family may not have agreed with his choice of a spouse; the name of the mother of his children is not recorded.

In January 1832, Harmon died in Twiggs County at Perryman's Mill, leaving a sizable estate, which in most cases would have been left to his wife Margaret and the children. Records are sketchy from this time period as to the children who are still in the county or state, and it is possible that Margaret has died. Thomas, the youngest, was named executor and was to see that his sister Harriet was given 250 acres, some slaves, and furniture. Thomas began to accumulate land on his own by being in the 1832 Georgia Land Lottery. Like his father, he became Justice of the Interior Court in Twiggs in 1832, 1834, and 1835. Records also show that a Thomas PERRYMAN served as private in the 37th Regiment of Georgia Cavalry, which was called into service for a short time in the Seminole Indian War in the Everglades. A cap ornament of an eight-pointed star was used in later years by veterans of that service, and some said Thomas often did the same.

In 1833, Thomas applied to sell land belonging to his father's estate. The legal entanglements went on for years. He continued to buy and sell land. For instance, in 1837, he and a partner bought land from Rebecca CAUDLE and then sold his half to his brother David. In the same year, the General Assembly of the State of Georgia named a group of Georgia residents, including Thomas, and stated that they were "hereby constituted in body corporate as the Jeffersonville Land Company of the County of Twiggs for the purpose of forming a village and erecting a female institution. The group shall not hold more land than a sufficient quantity of acres for a town." Thomas at this point had seventeen slaves, probably some given as part of his father's estate, and some he had traded or bought on his own.

Four years later in 1841, Thomas and Hardy DURHAM were named administrators for the estate of James LOWERY. Was he a father-in-law or uncle of the unrecorded earlier marriage? Whatever the connection, by the next year the heirs of the estate sued Thomas to recover their shares and were awarded $2045.64 each. The heirs next sued DURHAM, because Thomas had transferred "certain promissory notes to DURHAM." The court awarded $3380 and court costs to the heirs. It was a dizzying number of lawsuits and legal work on each side with both sides blaming the other for the confusion.

Thomas was still mentioned in a suit brought by LOWERY heirs back in Twiggs County, Georgia, which went all the way to the Georgia Supreme Court. Their ruling stated, "Because Perryman, before leaving the state, paid all or nearly all he owed, he had a credit of $11,000 to which he was entitled. He has already gone to Texas and took all his visible property. He had left a trunk with bills, bonds, promissory notes, titles to land valued at $8,000. He has given directions to pay off any amount due heirs and Durham has done so."

Thomas was usually such a good businessman that it seems strange that he would have left such loose ends unless he had planned the outcome to the penny and thought it was to his benefit to make the arrangements for the trunk. Leaving Georgia was certainly in his plan, so the trunk had its place in whatever arrangements he thought best. Thomas Perryman felt the call of the Texas Hill Country and moved his own group and all his possessions to this rough, developing, challenging Lone Star State.

Texas—a place of great land speculation in 1850 and possibilities that lured people from everywhere. Guadalupe County land was fine sandy loam with a growing season of at least 275 days a year. There would be plenty of space for farming, ranching, and raising horses with fewer than 1000 white residents in Lower Cibolo Valley. Slavery was allowed even though his German-born neighbors did not support the idea. He had the resources to acquire the land and to raise cattle and horses as he wanted to. The brand he chose was "TP" as his initials, so it would become a familiar mark to those around.

From 1838 Thomas made a number of changes in his life. He married Elisabeth S. WILLIS who was probably a wealthy widow with no children. The "S" was a maiden name that has never been established. They had their first child, Harriet Caroline, in 1840. In 1842, Thomas and his growing family moved to Alabama where his father and older brothers had land. His son William was born there. By 1846, he and the family were in Louisiana with the addition of daughter Ella. The family and all their possessions were in Washington County, Texas, and welcomed another son, Edward. With political and educational plans to make the area the most populous in Texas, the area became a bustling spot of activity. But by 1849, the PERRYMANS were residents of Guadalupe County, Lower Cibolo Valley, Texas, and acquired a large chunk of the grassy Hill Country land.

Fellow citizens in 1849 saw the business sense that PERRYMAN had and approached him to be an "agent with full powers on behalf of the county to receive subscription and donations to build a first-rate substantial jail." Maybe they thought he could persuade other land owners of the necessity of such a structure.

PERRYMAN was considered to be quite wealthy both in land and personal possessions. From 1850 to 1853, THOMAS continued to add to livestock. There were more horses and cattle with taxes paid on a herd of 400 cattle and 14 horses. He also added extra land, 640 acres each in plots near Santa Clara and Elm Creek.

His name appears in the Cherokee Land Lottery in Georgia where he had received land in his own name before coming to Texas. He was appointed as a County Commissioner in 1850 as well as overseer of a new road to San Antonio at the Cibolo crossing. Some even named him among the one hundred wealthiest Texans of the time. He was a charter member of the Cibolo Masonic Lodge organized in 1854. The group was made up of landowners in the area, and he was elected to several positions: Senior Warden, Junior Warden, and Treasurer three times. There were fifteen charter members, and they met at the Valley Post Office, which was Thomas' ranch, for the next eight years. Records for the Cibolo Masonic Lodge, No. 151 in 1857 report that T.J. PERRYMAN is a Master Mason, and J.B. BROWN is shown to be an entered Apprentice.

Few Germans held slaves at this time, but there were slave holders in the community. Thomas PERRYMAN had sixteen in 1850, forty-one in 1859, twenty-eight in 1860. W.W. ANDERSON had one, and James BURBANK had five. PERRYMAN's place was on the Seguin/San Antonio Road off Santa Clara Creek. He and his wife Elizabeth Willis PERRYMAN declared ownership of slaves, hers being separate property with seven slaves, two beds, one horse, and one hundred head of cattle.

This would have been slightly unusual for the time to declare her own possessions, but there is some speculation that she was his second wife, and the property could have been hers from her own family. Thomas PERRYMAN bought two slaves for $1200 in June 1859, a mother, and a two-year old son. That was the year of his largest number of slaves, forty-one at a value of $20,500. Elizabeth showed a record of twenty-four worth $14,400. The average dollar value of slaves in Texas during this time was approximately $765.

PERRYMAN's wife, Elizabeth, became postmistress of the Valley Post Office in 1866 as Thomas became more involved with cattle drives.

The 1850 census for the county reads:

#112 1850 UNITED STATES CENSUS
GUADALUPE COUNTY, TEXAS

THOMAS J. PERRYMAN 35 Farmer $10,000 b. Georgia
ELISABETH 30 b. Georgia
H. AUGUSTUS 18 Student b. Georgia
HARRIET 10 b. Georgia
WILLIAM 8 b. Alabama
ELLIE 4 b. Louisiana
EDWIN 2 b. Texas

Another son, Robert, was born just after the census was taken.

The tax evaluation for Thomas is based

on ownership of 1,004 acres, 16 Negro slaves, 11 horses, 158 cattle, and 800 sheep. Elisabeth had slaves in her own name at that time with as many as twenty-eight slaves ages one to forty. It was quite a large ranching/farming venture as seen by the tax evaluation.

ELISABETH had her own property and made sure it was noted: "ELISABETH S. PERRYMAN whose former name was Elisabeth S. Willis not wife of Thomas Perryman, desirous of securing to herself the property which she lawfully possessed at the time of her marriage, declares 7 slaves, 2 beds, 1 horse, and 100 head of cattle."

His second son, James, is not listed with the family in the household for 1850 in Texas and could be anywhere at this point. H. Augustus is still with the family but is probably attending college since he is shown to be a student and is eighteen. Baylor University started in Washington County, Texas, by this date, and since the family had once lived there, it would have been a logical college for a young man to attend and not be an impossible distance away.

The fall of 1854 was the beginning of a legal wrangle which would involve Thomas, his fellow Mason Robert RUSSELL, and Valley landowner Nathan BUSBY for more than a year. It all began when the three men were instructed to be on the Guadalupe County Slave Patrol based on a law passed in 1846 and one in 1853. Any slaves who were found to be using provocative language or menacing gestures to receive as much as thirty-six lashes. The slaves had to have a pass from their owners allowing them to move freely. Patrols had been introduced in South Carolina in 1784 to make slave owners vigilant against any slave uprisings. In Texas there were always threats that slaves would escape to Mexico or the West, so the patrols were meant to break up any slave meetings, apprehend runaways, or monitor any potential slave movements. By 1850 there were over 58,000 slaves in Texas with slave dealers in Galveston and Houston.

Guadalupe County set up slave patrols to include at least three to five men who were slave owners and would serve for three to six months. A captain, and at least two privates, were to patrol at least once each month. Because of their participation, the slave patrollers were sometimes exempt from county taxes or fees for that period. Slaves caught without a pass could receive twenty-five lashes although the law also allowed harsher amounts if the action seemed more serious. An old slave prayer said, "Oh, Lord, we thank you for the New Jerusalem with the pearly gates and the golden streets, but above all, we thank Thee for that high wall around the great big city, so high that the slave patrol can't get over it."

Thomas PERRYMAN, Robert RUSSELL, and Nathan BUSBY were on the Guadalupe Slave Patrol in the spring of 1853. BUSBY's family had been in Twiggs County, Georgia, about the same time as THOMAS. He owned two slaves and lived a peaceful life in the county. Fellow Mason Robert RUSSELL had four slaves and seemed respected by his neighbors even though the German-born residents of the county did not believe in slavery. They did, however, support states' rights. The incident which caused such a furor took place when the three were out on their patrol under the authority of the County Court.

Rumors had been swirling in the county that landowner James WEIR was allowing his slaves to travel without passes and was ignoring laws set by the county. There may have been some past run-ins with Thomas and other landowners. WEIR, an Irish-born land speculator named his Bexar County holdings as "Rancho de la Cibolo." He made a trip from Kentucky to Texas by steamboat down the Mississippi to New Orleans and then to Indianola and finally by wagon to Bexar County on the line next to Guadalupe County. Almost as soon as he arrived, he began legal entanglements with those around him about boundaries or mishaps. On his place twenty miles east of San Antonio, his twenty-five slaves were called "servants" to those who asked, even though they were not free, and his big "W" brand was all over his possessions. His job as postmaster for the Valley in 1852 may have put him at odds with Thomas who became the postmaster of the Valley after him and at his location rather than at WEIR's place.

This was the way the argument unfolded. A group of slaves were reported to be coming over in Guadalupe County from Bexar County and were said to be drinking. Who reported them? Not known. Why would they have flaunted themselves that way? Not known. The Patrol captured them, tied them up, and beat them. How many lashes? Not known for certain. But after a certain amount of time, they were sent back to Bexar County and to WEIR with a stern warning that it was not to happen again and a message that WEIR was to be admonished for not supervising his slaves (servants) in the proper way.

WEIR answered in time with a suit filed in Comal County. According to WEIR, one of the men "became lame and sick and unable to perform his usual labor and service for a month."

This began the paper suits and countersuits between WEIR and slave patrol members. He wanted compensation for lost labor and medical expenses because the Patrol "with force had assaulted, beat, bruised, injured, and maltreated" the slave. They had also committed a "similar assault on another slave and did great damage by lacerating the skin in several places."

The patrol answered by saying that WEIR's slaves were "roaming over the county at night" and were "to a great extent intoxicated" and were "armed with swords, knives, pistols, guns and other deadly weapons." The legal order was:

Filing date—October 16, 1854
Amended Petition—May 11, 1855
Interrogators—September 14, 1855
Answers to Interrogators—April 21, 1855
Amended Answer—May 11, 1855
Order of Court Record—April 19, 1855
Bill of Costs—June 1855

The result was, as expected, in favor of Thomas, RUSSELL, and BUSBY. Guadalupe County had been assigning patrols since 1849 and continued while the case was in court. There were at least six named for each patrol with as many as nine in one time period. THOMAS was first named a private but became the captain on all later patrols, so it is clear he was the captain on the WEIR slave patrol in the area designated as District 2. Patrol members at this time included JOHN WICKES, JOHN DURHAM, JOHN BURRESS, J.J. FRAZIER, RUDOLPH HELMAN, S.E. EDWARDS, JOHN DONALDSON, DAVID CURRIE, WILLIAM HINDS, and A.T. COOK.

There was no damage to Thomas PERRYMAN's reputation because of the incident, and he continued as postmaster for the Valley and received $29.69 in compensation for 1856 even though there was only $6.51 in revenue. He was named Overseer on the San Antonio Road by Erskine Ferry. It was his job to work the intersection of the road to Cibolo with all hands living in that area toward Santa Clara and Cibolo, subject to road duty and responsible for road repair. The Commissioner's Court required work on the roads, and those who did not help could be prosecuted, pay a fine, or pay the overseer for the time they did not work. The area of Zhuel on Cibolo Creek became known as PERRYMAN'S CROSSING. He also was presiding officer over elections held at this time.

PERRYMAN's son, H.A., a member of the Guadalupe County Masons, met in Seguin rather than with his father's group, probably because he was living and practicing law in Seguin. His advertisements in 1855 and 1856 stated: "H.A. PERRYMAN, attorney and counselor at law Seguin—Will give attention to the collection of debts, the prosecution of land claims—Office South side of Market Square."

Fast horses, a love Thomas had all his life, could hold his attention, and he participated in the Jockey Club established in Seguin. The first races held in 1854 became more organized with each year. Entry fee was $5.00 for the one-mile dash with a winner's purse of $150 on the first day's running and $300 on the second. It was an enjoyable time in Guadalupe County as cotton average had increased to over 9,000 acres and cattle numbered more than 40,000 head.

Thomas and Elisabeth continued to hold a high number of slaves to work the land and care for the livestock. In 1855 there were thirty-eight slaves on the tax roll, fifteen horses, and four hundred head of cattle. There were five hundred more cattle in 1857 and more horses, fifty-two. In 1859, Thomas bought two slaves, ADALINE and her baby for $1200. The entire slave population for Guadalupe County was 1,748 with 202 slave holders in the county, only three owners had more than forty slaves. Elisabeth listed her own slaves at twenty-four while Thomas showed thirty-five. In the county, there were 67,000 head of cattle, over 7,000 sheep, 12,000 horses, and 18,000 hogs.

The year 1860 was a dramatic time for everyone. Voters in Guadalupe County approved secession 314-22 even though the German-born voters were against slavery. They came from a place where the government took away their rights, so they felt that states had to protect themselves even in this issue. The PERRYMAN family had increased by now.

1860 UNITED STATES CENSUS
GUADALUPE COUNTY, TEXAS

PERRYMAN, Thomas J.	50	$25,000
Elisabeth	40	
Carrie	19	
William	17	
Ellen	14	
Eddy	12	
Robert	10	
Mattie	7	
Dejarnette	4	

Carrie, the oldest daughter in the family, became engaged to Mississippi-born and Ol' Miss graduate John Neville SIMMONS and married December 23, 1861. However, they were only together for a brief time before JOHN enlisted in the Confederacy and became aide-de-camp to his brother-in-law, General Thomas WAUL.

There was still work to be done even if the war was raging in the South. Elisabeth was post mistress for two years, 1861-1862 at the Valley Post Office which was once again their house. She was on the tax rolls for five slaves on one piece of property and twenty-three on another. THOMAS showed ownership of 1640 acres in the county, 1000 head of cattle, 600 sheep, and 18 slaves in his own name. A happy occasion was the birth of Carrie and John's son who they named, Thomas, after his grandfather.

But happiness for the new couple was displaced when word came that so many families on both sides of the War received. Carrie's husband, John Neville had been killed at the siege of Vicksburg between May 18 and July 4th. According to his brother-in-law, John "left an undying record of courage." It is probable he never saw his son.

A strange event took place on May 16, 1863 when a suit was brought against Thomas in Guadalupe District Court which stated that "THOMAS J. PERRYMAN late of said county on the first day of January A.D. 1863 and in diverse times from that day did place ten negro slaves in charge of a farm discharged and removed several miles from the said PERRYMAN has during said time failed to keep a free white person upon or in charge of said farm."

Someone must have complained to authorities or had a grudge against Thomas, but the charge had to be filed. Thomas did not settle but asked for a jury trial. On May 19 the jury found him guilty and assessed a fine of $50 which he was to pay immediately. It was a small matter compared to some difficulties that his German-born neighbors had encountered. Although Cibolo and Schertz had not had hangings or visits from vigilantes, some in the Hill Country had endured torments because of their political beliefs.

During the War, Thomas probably sold cattle and other provisions to the Confederate forces as other ranchers in the area did. Texas beef was necessary to feed the home guards and local militia. Longhorns were easy to raise because they were sturdy, and his herds had increased greatly. He had sold many of his sheep, but Elisabeth had more than 200 on her list for tax rolls. Horses were perhaps more important, more his favorites, and he also continued to buy and sell land. When the surrender came in 1865, THOMAS and some of his neighbors sent some small herds to the Red River Station in Montague County. Cattle were $4 a head in San Antonio but more than that farther north. This was about to make an enormous difference in the life of every rancher in Texas.

Stockyards were built in Abilene, Kansas, a place few people had heard of, but it would be a key to railroads transporting cattle to the beef-hungry North. The owner encouraged Texans to bring their cattle. The Old San Antonio Road had come straight through Guadalupe County since the days of Spanish exploration in the 1700s, so ranchers could imagine pushing the herds up the old pathway. Thomas sent his own cattle and was agent for numbers of others who were not sure how to organize the drive: a trail boss, ten cowboys, a cook, and a horse wrangler who would leave in the spring and arrive in Abilene in two months or so. They would follow the old Shawnee Trail as it headed north to Kansas. Starting with approximately 2,400 head of cattle, the goal was ten to twelve miles a day over the unfenced pastures as cattle grazed and moved at a slow pace. It was a huge gamble, and there were some who said it would not work. But the lure of $40 or more a head in Abilene was worth the risk to Thomas and the others. When they received word in early summer the first herd had arrived and been sold, "THOMAS PERRYMAN became one of the wealthiest men in Texas." And the trail—the name became the Chisholm Trail.

For the next four years Thomas continued to send herds north and to buy and sell land. William and Edward had moved from his house although they remained in Guadalupe County to help with the family business. H.A. continued with his law practice but moved to Louisiana. Things were running smoothly, and Thomas formed the PERRYMAN-LYTLE Cattle Company to push the herds north and even included some of the WURZBACH boys as cowboys. His sons might have made the trip and negotiated for his father in the sales of herds for $80,000 or more. Trail bosses continued to make $100 to $125 a month and cooks $60. Bonuses were a cowboy's dream as they watched each owner's brand and herd. But Thomas must have seen that so many cattle would eventually mean a flooded market, and he knew that he needed to look for other measures of profit.

In 1867, he joined with a group of shareholders in the purchase of a former distillery in New Braunfels and turned it into the New Braunfels Woolen Manufacturing Company (NBWMC). His partners were Franz MOUREAU, C.F. GROSS, Adolphe GIESCKE, and Julius GIESCKE. With starting capital of $40,000, they took the old building on the Comal River. They bought land and a grist mill at a cost of $9,000 so they would have a permanent supply of firewood on Waco Springs which had been called Guadalupe Springs. They bought spinning frames and looms for the two-story, 40' x 90' building with an 80' smokestack. Machinery cost $25,000, and the GIESCKE brothers would oversee day-to-day operations of the mill. Steam engines provided the power to produce blankets and other woolen items. The plant furnished 1,233 yards of gray wool cloth to Texas A and M for uniforms. At its peak, NBWMC could make 200 yards of twee or yarn, 40 pairs of blankets a day, and often won first prize in national contests.

Major problems with the company was the need for 600-700 pounds of wool daily and the competition of other manufacturing activity in the area. It was true that New Braunfels was a bustling town with thirty dry goods stores, three flour mills, three saw mills, mechanic shops, a sash facility, a cotton cloth factory, and a growing population. Its location was a good one. Thomas was certainly aware that money could be made in several areas as the city grew. With that in mind, he made the decision to move from Cibolo to New Braunfels with his remaining children, his widowed daughter, and grandson.

1870 United States Census
Comal County

PERRYMAN, THOMAS	55	$20,000 (personal value)
		$100,000 (land value)
ELISABETH	52	
ELLEN	20	
ROBERT	17	
MATTY	15	
JANETTE	13	
CARRIE	27	
THOMAS	8	

Although the business was successful, it didn't seem to hold the attention of Thomas like ranching and racing had. In 1874, he and the other shareholders decided to move on to other enterprises. They transferred the property and its indebtedness to the GIESCKE brothers for $18,265. Why such a low number? There is not an explanation, so there may have been some other business moves not recorded in the sale. The three hundred spindles and the broad blanket looms would continue a little longer, but Thomas was not involved. He still bought and sold land and maintained his holdings in Guadalupe County as he now lived in New Braunfels. For three years, there is no record of any other business investment he made which is a long time for Thomas to remain out of any planning. A street in New Braunfels was named for him perhaps at this point.

On February 1, 1877, THOMAS died. Was it a sudden death after a brief illness? A heart attack? The result of a longer illness? Nothing remains to tell us of that. The Austin-American Statesman, a newspaper in Austin, reported, "THOMAS J. PERRYMAN of New Braunfels, is no more. He lived many years on the Cibolo in Guadalupe County." Why would an Austin newspaper put the notice in its paper? Three years earlier, at about the time in 1874 when Thomas was getting out of the woolen business, he made a will. He appointed his "beloved wife, ELISABETH" as the executrix with witnesses

Henry SCHOLL and Adam SCHOLL.

The will, which Thomas made out is perhaps strangely worded in some respects. His son, H.A. (Harmon Augustus) is mentioned first despite being second-born and is given $15 "in addition to what he has already acquired." The small amount of money could be in addition to land he was given earlier or the two slaves before the War or money or the price of his son's education or anything that comes to mind. THOMAS next leaves $50 each to the "heirs of my son JAS. L. PERRYMAN," so there is the strong possibility that his oldest son is dead. How many heirs were there? Had contact been so limited that THOMAS could not name his grandchildren at this time? James certainly had not lived close to Thomas since before the move to Texas. Thomas then authorizes Elisabeth to take charge of the estate, pay any debts, and manage the estate in the best interest of their heirs, and "as each child becomes of age or marriage to allow them such an amount as she thinks best." Second, at the point he wrote the will Carrie, William, Edward, Ellen, Robert, and Matty would all have been considered of age with Dejarnette almost seventeen, so why the wording of the statement?

The estate was sizable as would be expected. It included in the inventory made in March and April of 1877:

- A tract of land in Comal County (10 acres)

- 2/3 interest in land in Coryell County (1,280 acres)
- ½ interest in land in Guadalupe County (1,400 acres)
- Interest in land in Kendall County (known as King Ranch)
- ½ of 1/3 in 6 lots of land in Monmouth, Warren County, Illinois
- ½ of 1/3 interest in land in Cass County, Nebraska (370 acres)
- Interest in the Western G Railway (no specific amount given)
- 2 notes against A.L. KESSLER who owns a general store and bank (each $4,105)
- 2 notes against New Braunfels Woolen Company ($1,000 ea)
- 1 note against A. NEILL who is a stockman ($400)
- 4 notes against LOUIS MATTOX, a clerk in Bexar County
- JOHN KALNA (3 notes for $200 and 1 for $72)
- 1 note against AUGUST BLACK ($157.50)
- 1 note against JOHN KEY who is a farmer ($150)

It seems, then, that THOMAS was loaning money to various people at all levels. His estate also names his possessions which were: 1 Durham buss, 1 carriage, 1 wagon, and a deposit in A.L. KESSLER Bank for $520.88 which would be worth approximately $11,000 in 2015 money. There is no listing of the house. The out-of-state real estate is interesting because land was cheap in these areas after the Civil War, so perhaps Thomas was planning another big venture in these spots.

Elisabeth did all the legal filings she was supposed to do and buried Thomas in a New Braunfels cemetery as she probated the will. Then after a short period of time she moved to Austin to property two miles from the capital. She had lived in New Braunfels for at least eight years and had been in the area of Cibolo since 1849, so the move to Austin may have been something that she and Thomas had been preparing for. Would he have been involved in politics? In the railroads that were coming to Texas? In something else that he saw as promising in the future of the area? With the history that he had of making money, it is certain that he would not have just watched any growth that was going on. And maybe he saw something in Austin that would be of more benefit than living in New Braunfels. Elisabeth, together with what family was left, moved and lived in a large house and enjoyed an easy lifestyle.

1880 UNITED STATE CENSUS
TRAVIS COUNTY, TEXAS

PERRYMAN, E.S.	60	
SIMMONS. C.	35	(Daughter)
ELLA	25	
MATTIE	23	
DEJARNETTE	21	
SIMMONS, T.J.	18	(Grandson)

There are no live-in servants listed, but it is likely they had full-time help.

On January 27, 1885, eight years after the death of her husband, Elisabeth died at the family home after a bout with pneumonia. Her children picked her burial spot in Oakwood Cemetery and three months later had their father's remains brought from New Braunfels and put beside her. Two of the children would also be buried there later.

Thomas PERRYMAN came to Cibolo Valley and made his mark on the community. There is no monument to him or highway named for him, no real notice that he became one of the wealthiest men on record. He came at a time when the state of Texas would be changed forever, and he felt the changes in his own world. His life showed the energy and will for success that marked the early days of Cibolo Valley.

CHILDREN OF THOMAS PERRYMAN

JAMES L.—mentioned in will; probably deceased by 1874

HARMON AUGUSTUS—1850 census at age 18 in Guadalupe County, Texas; in Seguin, Texas as lawyer through 1856; in Bienville Parish, Louisiana census in 1870; argued cases in district court of Louisiana through 1872.

CARRIE—in 1850 census of Guadalupe County, married JOHN NEVILLE SIMMONS on December 20, 1860; in 1870 census of Comal County living with parents and son; in 1910 census with sister ELLA FENNER.

WILLIAM—was in 1850 and 1860 census of Guadalupe County; in 1880 census of Guadalupe County with wife, KATE, two children, and brother EDWARD.

ELLA—in 1850 and 1860 census of Guadalupe County; in 1870 census of Comal County; in 1880 census of Travis County; married VIRGIL FENNER, partner in Be Jones Printing through 1897; died in 1932 in Travis County.

MATTIE—in 1860 census of Guadalupe County; in 1870 census of Comal County; in 1880 census of Travis County; married Mr. MATTHEWS; buried in Austin, Travis County, Texas.

EDWARD—in 1860 and 1880 census in Guadalupe County; married LOUISE ASHER; in 1900, 1910, 1920 census in Gonzales County; died in

Caldwell County, Texas in 1925.

ROBERT—in 1860 census Guadalupe County; in 1870 census Comal County; married EMMA CROSS in 1878; buried in Austin, Travis County, Texas.

DEJARNETTE—in 1860 census Guadalupe County; 1870 census Comal County; in 1880 census of Travis County, Texas.

THOMAS—in 1862 census; 1870 census Comal County.

THOMAS DAVID PERRYMAN
buried Fort Sam Houston
b. 13 Oct 1843 b. buried 14 Oct 1843 Plot P-C 196
Infant son of THOMAS L. PERRYMAN, Jr.
1st LT 86th Navigation Tng GP

THE CHISHOLM TRAIL

PERRYMAN not only had crops on his land but also a large herd of cattle. He saw the value in investing in the first trail drive to send cattle with his big "TP" brand to the northern shipping points and added to his worth. His brand was among the 35 listed for the Valley in 1865, so the cattle were there. The Chisholm Trail began at the Rio Grande around 1866 and continued through Dewitt County to Cibolo, Austin, Round Rock, Georgetown, and on to Kansas. Crossings were on the Colorado River near Austin, Brushy Creek near Round Rock, Kimball's Bend on the Brazos, and Trinity Ford near Fort Worth. The most favorable size for a herd was 2500 to 3000 cattle, and the herd and drivers could cover 10-15 miles a day. No one had attempted the drives before this time, but there was a demand for beef in the northern states, and those who were willing to gamble on the success of a drive could make a great deal of money. In 1866, for instance, cattle sold for $5 while in 1867 the price had risen to $9.50 in Texas and double or triple that amount in the North.

Forgotten Roads and Texas Travelers

Gonzales to San Antonio
Guadalupe County

It was probably animals who made the first path going east to west through the area. White tailed deer, coyotes, bobcats, and maybe even bison herds. Even nine-banded armadillo could have joined the parade. It had no name at this time, but the water of the creek that was near it was clear and sweet.

Next came the Lipan Apache, Tonkawa, Wichita, Comanche, and a few Caddo whose chief had to try to exist with the larger tribes surrounding his people. It was always the water they used as a boundary, sometimes pushing the bison over the steep banks for an easy kill. They also shared the land with the Coahuiltecan tribes to the south and made uneasy alliances in most cases when the fierce Comanches showed who was the most feared. They had scattered villages of teepees and fished in the waters. It was not such a difficult place to camp even in the winters because the temperatures were never so low.

Becoming adept at smoke signals and the use of the lance, the Sun Otter Band of Lipan Apaches settled along Cibolo Creek, not far from where Cibolo (Selma) was located from about 1750. Another band of the Apaches, the Lower Lipans, were headed by Chief FLACCO. He became well known and was associated with Texas Ranger "Jack" Coffee HAYES. He described FLACCO as "tall and erect with well-shaped limbs—gave an impression of boding activity—with black eyes and a bearing of fierce alertness with strength and agility." HAYES said that FLACCO had saved his life several times in battles with the Comanches.

Leaders for the Sun Otters, Cuelgas de CASTRO and later Ramon CASTRO and Juan CASTRO, were often mistaken for Comanche. These chiefs had received the surname of "CASTRO" from the military commander of the northeastern provinces from 1787-1792. Their bison camp became known as LIPAN OLD TOWN, and they did more planting than some of the other tribes. An Indian agent in the 1840s reported "The Lipan are anxious to be settled and will plant corn and grain this year on the Cibolo at the Old Town."

The area was said to have remains of the buried dead which would be typical of the LIPANS since they normally located a village near the burial place of their dead. It was considered a spiritual part of who they were. They still used the cliffs of the Cibolo to hunt bison.

A later resident of the area whose land was next to Old Town, William DAVENPORT, described it in this way: "The cliffs are white with caves in them. I watched in surprise as the Apache men ran the bison over the side of the cliffs to fall on the rocks below."

But, this practice was not used just on the Cibolo. It was a common way to kill bison throughout the Southwest and was often called "bison jumps" by any number of tribes. It had proved to be effective, so most Indians used it as a first resource.

Tonkawas were never considered a major tribe by the other Indians, maybe because they were even more nomadic than their counterparts. Some said their name meant "they all stay together" because their origin was from several different groups. They called themselves the "real people," and they initially were sworn enemies of the Apache. Later they concentrated efforts against the Comanche and joined with the Apache. They were great hunters and depended entirely on the bison rather than trying to be planters. Slender, fast, able to go for long periods on horse without food or water, they gained a reputation as being very skilled. But, by 1803 some writers could only count 200 warriors in the area of Cibolo Creek. They gradually diminished from disease and attacks from other Indians.

Some early reports and diaries referred to

the water as the CIVVILLO or CIBOLO. It may have meant "bison" in one of the Indian dialects. Names for it were varied. The Coahuiltecan said it was "Xolota." The Tonkawas called it "BataConiquiyoquo." In 1691 Father Damian MASSAN gave it the name "Santa Creceanan," while Domingo TERAN de los RIOS wrote of the San Ynacio de Loyola. "San XAVIER" was the name used by Domingo RACHO. However, the Spanish who came called it the Cibolo River.

ALARCON's 1718 expedition mentioned the Cibolo Creek but said it was a strong water with hackberries, live oaks and elms lining it. In 1721 it was the "Arroyo del Cibolo" to Marques de SAN MIGUEL DE AGAYO. In 1791 Joseph de AZLAR y VORTA de VERA wrote of crossing the Cibolo after he had been in San Antonio and moved northward. It was, however, the Gonzales to San Antonio Road which received most of the traffic and Spanish troop movement.

Byrd LOCKHART (1782-1839), had to deal with the numbers who used the road as he walked through mesquite and wild grapes not far from the Cibolo. As surveyor, he left crude mile markers carved on tree trunks where it was passable.

LOCKHART's survey crossed the Cibolo south of the crossing that would come to be known as BROWN's and went north and south of the Crescent Bend. It was usually called the Upper San Antonio Road although sometimes it was the Wood

Road because of the number of the timbers hauled from east to west.

Before LOCKHART got to Texas, he had already seen action of various kinds. In 1814 in Madison County, Illinois, he and Zachary TAYLOR (Old "Rough and Ready") were indicted along with one other man in the assault of a French-American. There was the hint that the man might have given some aid to the British in the War of 1812, but no proof exists of that today. At any rate, the assault was ignored until 1818 when TAYLOR and the others were charged again. TAYLOR was found not guilty, but that was not the case for LOCKHART who was found guilty. He and his family hastily left the state, and he became one of the earliest surveyors in Arkansas. In 1826 with the lure of land and a new start, he became an assistant to Green DEWITT in the surveying necessary for DEWITT's Colony. Five years later, the Mexican Governor of the territory named him the official surveyor.

As a surveyor, LOCKHART had to watch for snakes, coyotes, unhappy land owners, and all manner of obstacles. He based his work on the plan devised by Stephen F. AUSTIN which was a system of surveying adjusting to the surveying chains of Mexico, slightly different from those in the United States. It was said later that he even made some road improvements and paid for them out of his own pocket. But he was a rugged individual who had settled in the Texas territory with DEWITT's

Colony in 1826 as a widower and was not afraid of danger. He told Stephen F. AUSTIN in a letter in 1830, "I can settle in a short time very much of this prairie country if you should please to have it done this way," and AUSTIN did. LOCKHART was in demand as a surveyor, and the Mexican government gave him four leagues of land on Plum Creek as payment for his services, then faced him as an enemy as he became a courier and spy for the Texan forces in the revolution.

He was at the Alamo but left with others to get supplies in Gonzales shortly before SANTA ANNA and his men attacked. A delay caused the group to be unable to help the besieged men, so he was saved from the fate of those who were there.

He worked with General HOUSTON in every way he could. His company of Mounted Riflemen were called on in 1835 to protect the frontier from Indian threats, for which he received $25 monthly, ammunition, and rations.

At his discharge in 1836, a fellow soldier remarked, "Our indefatigable Ranger, Captain Byrd LOCKHART has returned to camp and reports the corn in the neighborhood of Bexar to be remarkable, fine and abundant and that several thousand bushels will be the result." Sadly, he only lived until 1839, but would have certainly been called on to do more surveying on Texas roads.

The Gonzales to San Antonio Road was as active as any spot could be during the Texas fight for rights to be an independent republic. SANTA ANNA had crossed the Cibolo below Martinez Creek as he shuffled troops. Mexican forces had gone to Gonzales in 1835 to get a cannon from townspeople, and the battle between the groups became a symbol for how Texans felt about the Mexican government. The residents of Gonzales and nearby communities refused to give up the cannon, so the Mexican army was forced to withdraw in this first battle. Reinforcements to the Alamo came down the road as they entered San Antonio. A story was often told that David CROCKETT and a small number of men went to the Cibolo and waited for any other group that might be coming from the north before heading back, knowing that help was not on its way.

Following the fall of the Alamo Susana DICKINSON and other survivors met a group of HOUSTON's men at Cibolo Crossing to tell what had happened at the battle and to relate that none of the men had gotten out alive. It is quite likely that SANTA ANNA and his staff traveled this road on March 31, 1836 toward an expected victory. Two battalions of soldiers, five pieces of artillery, and rations all lumbered along. Erastus "Deaf" SMITH (1787 – 1837) was said to have spied on Mexican forces from a perch in a tall tree on the Cibolo, so he could report numbers and troop divisions to HOUSTON. The Gonzales to San Antonio Road was marked by soldiers, survivors, and heroes.

After Texas won its right to be independent

from Mexico, DEAF SMITH was awarded a land grant on the northeast side of Cibolo Creek. The crossing was one of only a few spots that could be used by wagons, so people often used it as they went across the Cibolo which ran a mile and a half in width in most places. Next to his land was land that had belonged to Vicente DURAN. DEAF SMITH had married DURAN's widow, Guadalupe Ruiz DURAN in 1822. She was a Tejana or Latino Texan who gave SMITH entry into the culture of that group. He was accepted by both Anglo and Tejana families.

A short time later, SMITH sold the lower half of his land including the crossing to LOCKHART. Although LOCKHART was a Texas Ranger in early 1837, he resigned his position and moved to Richmond where he died. He had only lived in Texas for fifteen years, but he made his mark on the country and the Cibolo.

A truly big announcement had been made in 1835 that would have an impact on the Gonzales to San Antonio Road and Guadalupe County. The United States Congress authorized mail contracts crisscrossing all of Texas. It was a type of courier service at first on horseback, but the sealed bids had been delivered to the office of the Post Master General of Texas, John JONES, in San Felipe de Austin. By the beginning of 1836, Route 14 would go from "Gonzales by Sandies and the Cibolo to Bejar, seventy-six miles once in two weeks." It would leave Gonzales at 7:00 a.m. every other Thursday and arrive the next Saturday at 7:00 p.m. in San Antonio.

In 1837, the first multi-passenger stage coaches took to the roads, and big cumbersome wagons would only be used rarely for freight. The Texas Legislature in 1842 passed an act to organize the County of Guadalupe with the Old Gonzales Road as the southern boundary. Four years later in 1846, the boundary was changed to a point farther down the Cibolo. The same year, Bexar County Commissioners authorized a new route using the old Gonzales Road to San Antonio by way of Claiborne RECTOR's house near Post Oak (later LaVernia), then leaving that road and going south along the west bank of the Cibolo.

Alabama-born Claiborne RECTOR came to Texas in 1830 and quickly became involved in the fight for independence. He served in the spy unit with Byrd LOCKHART and was at the battle of San Jacinto. For his service, he received a 4,000-acre land grant, and there he established a blacksmith's shop.

Two young businessmen, one originally from Scotland and one from New York, began a partnership to move passengers and mail across Texas. Thirty-two-year-old John B. BROWN (sometimes referred to as John F. or I.T. or even James because of illegible handwriting) and thirty-seven-year-old Lyman TARBOX began an operation out of Houston to WASHINGTON-ON-

THE-BRAZOS, a thirty-hour trip which began at the Houston House Inn. It was considered a truly innovative way to journey instead of by horseback. Now BROWN and TARBOX could be called "stagers," the nickname for those who had a stage company.

Where were they before they got into the stagecoach/mail business? TARBOX was listed as a Fourth Corporal in the supply section of Captain DANIEL's Military Guard of 1838-39, the well-armed Milam Guards coming out of Houston to fight the Indians on the Little Brazos River. The Guards were the first recorded military unit to fight after Texas received its independence and were limited to seventy-five men who provided their own tents, wagons, and camp equipment. They were used as escorts for frontier guards in Indian raids and carried flintlock muskets. Their gray uniforms with black trim and white metal buttons were completed with a dark blue cap. TARBOX is listed with the company as one of a jury that decided on the charge of murder of one guard by another. After evidence was heard, the jury decided on a verdict of accidental discharge of a rifle. So, he would have been in Texas by at least 1837 and probably in Houston.

A John BROWN is listed with Captain BRISCO's Rangers at the same time, and the units fought together, but there is no proof that TARBOX and BROWN might have met this way. An even more likely listing is that of "John BROWN, 1st

Infantry, Army of the Republic of Texas, enlisted for three years on Nov. 11, 1839, Galveston, age twenty-seven, height 5 ft. 2 in., fair complexion, blue eyes, dark hair, carpenter by trade, born in Ireland." BROWN classified himself as a veteran in later years. A family record for him describes him as a "quartermaster" and related that he participated in the battle of Monterey in 1846, but this would have been when he was running his hotel and stage lines and might only have meant he supplied stock.

Did BROWN come through Texas first at Galveston or Victoria? Perhaps. An interesting listing for a ship coming to Philadelphia from Londonderry, Ireland, in 1834 shows a nineteen-year-old John BROWN who is a shoemaker. A land grant in March 1839 and in Victoria in May 1845 would fit a ship coming from the East Coast.

TARBOX had made claims for reimbursement or restitution for his military experience and received a land grand in Bell County for his service. For a short time, he kept a horse for the government. It earned him $10.50. In 1840 he had one poll for tax purposes in Brazoria County. In 1845, he was paid $5 for the feeding of a Bay Horse and Grey Pony that had been used for some cash given to Indian Jim SHAW. Another $10 is issued for further service to the War Department. A voucher was given for his salary as an Indian agent. His trade with Indian Jim was part of a policy that had been encouraged in 1841 by President Sam HOUSTON who wanted to establish agents not trying to go to battle with the Indians but instead to trade with them and encourage them to make peace with the settlers. President Anson JONES also continued the policy, so it is likely that TARBOX moved among the Comanches and Tonkawas who were along the Cibolo. Battles still took place, but they were less frequent than before the attempt to trade.

In 1845 BROWN delivered goods as a freighter to the Indian Bureau. A bill was recorded to show he was owed $2.50 for freighting of a package for 75 cents, a box of candles for $1.00 and two kettles for 75 cents. The items had been bought from Messrs. TORREY in Houston for the Indian Bureau. Anson JONES, last president of the Republic of Texas, wrote a letter in September 1845 that he had loaned a mule to "Mr. BROWN, the stage proprietor." An ad in early 1845 for a stage from Houston to Washington with the contract for mail "will run with a carriage to accommodate passengers. J.F. BROWN." "Limpy" reported his nickname came about as a result of some Indian battle; it was not an unbelievable event in that time. Fights occurred on the Cibolo in 1843 with the Comanche that involved several Texas men.

He was known as a hotel owner in Victoria of one of the three hotels there and possibly a smaller one in Houston. The value of the Victoria Hotel, one of his competitors, was $1500 in a sale, and BROWN's place was larger and acted as a stage stop when stage lines were developed. In 1846 the ad for BROWN's HOTEL noted the changes that had been made.

BROWN'S HOTEL

The undersigned begs to inform his friends, and the public generally that he has repaired and put in order the house built by BENNETT and PRESCOTT and is now ready to receive and entertain in the best manner those who may favor him with a call.

Board per week without lodge – $14.00
Board per week with lodging – $15.00
Breakfast – 37 cents
Dinner – 50 cents
Supper – 37cents
Lodging – 25 cents
Horse feed – 25 cents

However, by the end of 1846, BROWN needed cash and put his hotel up for sale. The sale notice listed details describing the building and would probably be a model for any later place he might have. It was nothing small or shabby according to this ad.

VALUABLE HOTEL STAND
FOR SALE

The undersigned, anxious to change his business, offers for sale the valuable and well-known establishment,

BROWN'S HOTEL, Victoria, Texas together with all its appurtenances.

The main building is a large two-story frame, well-arranged for hotel purposes, and now in complete order—having recently undergone on through repairing. It has a fine large dining room, two fireplaces, and a neat barroom; and has connected with it a superb frame kitchen, wash house, also on the premises, a substantial newly erected storeroom which is now rented for six months at $20 per month. The premises occupy two entire lots upon which is a fine garden well paled in and attached to the Hotel.

Also—a large and substantial two-story stable, capable of holding horses. The stable is in complete order and has attached to it a horse lot. The establishment has a fine run of profitable as can be attested by any person who has visited Victoria. The purchaser can have the entire furniture and fixtures of the Hotel at a fair valuation should he desire them.

The above premises will be sold cheap should the application be made soon. One or two good servants with the balance in cash would be received in payment. He would return grateful thanks to those who have so liberally patronized him on this place, and at the same time assure them that so long as he continues to cater for their appetites, he will spare no pain to please.

He would take this occasion to remind them who have claims against him to present them for settlement; as also to request those indebted to him to make payment immediately as he is settling up his business.

The ad ran in three papers: Victoria, Galveston, and Matagorda. Matagorda was the smallest of the three but had a steady flow of immigrants coming in as the other did, so perhaps BROWN thought someone would be ready for an investment in a new land. There must not have been a reasonable offer to businessman BROWN, and the Hotel continued to function with his name attached for at least another two years.

Travelers gave his name in several of their journals. Mrs. Amanda DIGNOWITY wrote in her remembrances of growing up that "Limpy Brown, well known in Texas history, kept the hotel in Victoria." Emily Brackett KING in a letter to her family said the same thing. Another early traveler to the area said that "Limpy Brown's stage stop was the uppermost settlement on the Cibolo" and that "he was a gentleman of high education and standing." In February 1847, BROWN again advertised his lodging as a fine place for people to frequent on their journeys. He also notes the trouble he has gone through to make the place better than before.

PRICES REDUCED
BROWN'S HOTEL

The undersigned begs to inform his friends and the public generally that he has repaired and put in complete order the house built BENNETT and PRESCOTT and is now ready to receive and entertain in the best manner those who may favor him for a call.

He has in addition a large and well-arranged stable

which will be consistently supplied with corn and provider. In short, he is determined that neither pains nor expense shall be spared to render his patrons as comfortable as possible.

In February 1848, BROWN was still in stiff competition with the other hotel owners in Victoria since it was a busy place for people coming into Texas or moving about the state. He again placed an ad in the Victoria paper to tell people that he had made great improvements in his hotel that would make them want to stay with him.

PRICES REDUCED
BROWN'S HOTEL

The undersigned takes pleasure in informing his old friends and the public generally that his home having recently undergone these rough repairs and having been well supplied with new and elegant furniture in every department, he is now fully prepared to accommodate all who may favor him with their business in a manner unsurpassed by any home in the State.

He has made very considerable additions to his former building and is now prepared to accommodate families with comfortable private rooms. He has just completed an excellent bath house which adjoins his building and is convenient of access. He is also completing a large cistern and well so that it will be all times abundantly supplied with good fresh water. His table will always be supplied with the best the market affords which will be served up in the best manner as he has excellent chosen and attentive servants.

He has in addition a large and well-arranged stable and horse lot, plenty of provender and good attentive hostlers.

John B. Brown

Somehow, the two men decided to form a partnership in the new business of moving people and goods from one point to another. BROWN was known to charge the same amount for a meal for a horse as a person, 25 cents. The first stage line he probably ever tried was one that left Victoria and went to Indian Point (Indianola) and then returned, all for the price of $2.50 or ten cents a mile. Now he was taking a partner and going after much longer routes. An ad in an 1845 Houston paper noted that the TARBOX and BROWN Stage from Houston would forward small packages in Express boxes for 50 cents each. Their notices continued through 1845 and into 1846. When they won the first annual federal contract for a thousand dollars to operate two-horse coach service between Austin and San Antonio, they could add that to the remarkable number of roads they would serve. On February 22, 1847, their ad in the *Houston Telegraph and Texas Register* said they would deliver mail from Houston to San Antonio. At least two routes existed which were passable for coaches: LaGrange to Bastrop, Austin, and San Antonio or LaGrange to Gonzales, Seguin, New Braunfels, and San Antonio. Trying to go a straight route to Houston was impossible because no freight had gone that way. In an advertised display also in the Houston Telegraph and Texas Register, BROWN noted, "The subscriber having the contract for carrying mail will run regularly with a carriage to accommodate passengers."

The stage left Houston at 6:00 a.m. and thirty hours later reached Washington-on-the-Brazos. In November 1847, they inaugurated the United States Stage Line between Port LaVaca and Victoria. Then they extended the route to a four-horse weekly service to New Braunfels via Cuero, Gonzales, and Seguin. They could use the old Gonzales to San Antonio Road on the Cibolo and then by a series of stage stops use the old Mill Road as it was called to Seguin. Their route connected with the Houston stage at Gonzales and the San Antonio to Austin line at New Braunfels. The Texas State Legislature had mandated the creation of "first class roads" between county seats. Forty feet should be the width of these roads. Small stumps less than eight inches could be cut at ground level. Large stumps were to be rounded off, so stages could pass. Second and third-class roads were twenty- and thirty-feet widths – IF a county could be pressed to get the roads finished to the specifications.

Not all those who rode their stage line were happy with their service. A lawsuit filed by a disgruntled customer, John S. KENNON, made it all the way to the Texas Supreme Court in winter of 1848 (with John being named as James and the initial used as "F" rather than "B").

> Lyman TARBOX and James F. BROWN
> Plaintiff in Error vs. John S. KENNON
> Defendant in Error
> Supreme Court of Texas
> December 1848

WRIT OF ERROR FROM HARRIS COUNTY

This suit was brought by the defendant in Error against the plaintiffs in error as common carriers to recover damages for the loss of goods which they had undertaken for transportation.

The goods were alleged to consist in a trunk and its contents claimed to have been the value of two hundred dollars. The plaintiffs recovered a verdict for fifty dollars. The defendant moved in arrest of judgement, the court overruled the motion, and the defendant sued once again.

The court found in favor of the lower court.

By 1848 HARRISON and MCCULLOUGH were also building stage routes in the area. Their advertisement in the December 29, 1848 Galveston Weekly News showed that they were not afraid to compete with BROWN and TARBOX as well as others and started their own line beginning in Galveston. "The U.S. Mail leaves the Planter's House on the arrival of steamers from New Orleans and Galveston by which travelers will have a speedy and direct route to Victoria, Cuero,

Gonzales, Seguin, New Braunfels, San Antonio, and Austin. Messrs. HARRISON and MCCULLOUGH, the well-known proprietors of the line, have placed upon it an excellent coach." In Cuero they could use Daniel FRIAR's home which served as a post office, store, and stage stop through 1849 until Crockett CARDWELL bought it.

That same year, Viktor BRACHT, a German-born businessman and explorer, wrote of his time in the hill country and the travels he had made. His book Texas in 1848 became a success both in Germany and the U.S. He made a ringing endorsement for the HARRISON and MCCULLOUGH line, probably because it was cheaper.

Many of the Texas roads are traveled regularly by mail coaches. Thus, BROWN and TARBOX's stage goes four times a week for Houston via Washington and Bastrop to Austin. The fare for the entire distance is twenty dollars, but only thirty pounds of baggage is carried free. Two competing stage lines make at least two weekly round trips to Bexar via New Braunfels and Victoria to Port LaVaca where they make connection with the steamboat to Galveston. I can recommend the stage coaches of MCCULLOUGH and HARRISON. The fare is ten dollars, and very little is charged for baggage.

BROWN must have continued as best he

could with the management of the hotel in Victoria. Although the ad for his hotel in 1848 said he had recently made improvements and the place was open for business, an ad in early part of 1849 reported the hotel "will be re-opened on Monday next for the reception of Boarders and Travelers." If the hotel sold, it did so by the end of the year. There are no ads for Brown's Hotel in the 1850 Victoria newspapers.

The busy world of 1849 Houston helped the BROWN and TARBOX stage line become a profit. Economic markers showed that "the streets of Houston have been completely crowded with wagons for the past three or four weeks. Goods to the amount of over a million dollars have been sent to the interior." And when they made the trip in an incredible time, the paper noted that. "New records in stagecoach travel was established by the driver of a BROWN and TARBOX coach who drove from Austin to Houston in thirty-six hours."

TARBOX was very involved with the world of Austin in its growth in 1850. He hosted a July 4th celebration along with John J. GRUMBLES on Barton Creek that had over 210 in attendance, so he made sure that barbecue was used as an advertisement for the stage line. Before that, he had been listed as a "patrolman" for the county. This meant that he was appointed by County Commissioners to be on the slave patrol based on a law passed first in 1846. Any slaves found using provocative language or menacing gestures that were a threat to the slave owners could get as much as thirty-six lashes.

A pass from their owners would allow them to move freely. In Texas there was always the possibility that slaves would escape to Mexico or go further West, so the patrols were formed to break up any slave plans for movements. By 1850 there were over 58,000 slaves in the state. A patrol could have three to five men and be in service for four to six months. Slave patrollers would sometimes be exempt from county taxes for the period that they served.

The papers in Texas ran notices of escaped slaves in almost every edition with the headline of "$50 Reward" and the name and description of the slave. They were held in the county jail until the owner could come for them, and if no one came in six months, the slave would be sold at public auction. Usually it was one slave.

RUNAWAY

On Sunday night the 7th, the Negro man ABRAM, near six feet, copper-colored, and about forty years of age. ABRAM is rather intelligent, handy in the use of tools, and a good carpenter and shoemaker. More details and the offer to pay a reward.

FIFTY DOLLARS REWARD

Runaway from Cherokee County, DAVE, age 28, about five feet ten inches,

> Weighs some 165 pounds, slow-speaking and
> smart, reads print tolerably well.
> He will likely aim for Mexico.

But the biggest fear that most slave patrollers had was a group who were making their way to the border.

> $200.00 REWARD
>
> Runaway from the residence of the
> Undersigned four miles east of Pine
> Bluff in Freestone County. Four Negroes.
> BOB, a yellow boy twenty, has a long,
> Bushy head of hair has an impudent,
> Sulky appearance—
> HENRY, twenty-two, pleasant and humble—
> MELINDA, hear eighteen, pleasant but bold
> OSCAR, twenty-four or twenty-five, no description

TARBOX is listed in the 1850 Slave Schedule as the owner of one fourteen-year-old boy. In Bexar County John BROWN is also listed as owning one boy of sixteen but was not shown on a patrol. Though he had come to America from Ireland where the Slave Trade Act for the British Empire had passed in 1807 abolishing the actual trading of slaves, he had found it too easy to buy a person on the Houston slave market or to receive one as part of a business arrangement.

Most of the travels were meant for the mail rather than the passengers. That was where the real money was to be made. There were many tales of discomfort. One rider wrote of paying money for his trip before knowing that the roads were really muddy from recent rains. He had to walk behind the coach for much of the way and help pull it out of any mud holes. Governor Sam HOUSTON also described a trip where the roads were terrible. In a letter to a friend, he wrote, "My trip was thro' awful roads. They were about as bad as they could be. On tomorrow I hope to reach Tiger Point and return direct to Houston."

BROWN and TARBOX had mail lines from Port Lavaca to San Antonio by way of Victoria, Gonzales, Seguin, and New Braunfels. A ticket on a bi-weekly stage route from Austin to Houston could be purchased for $20 fare which included 30 lbs. of luggage. Any extra luggage was six cents a pound. The trip usually took at least two and a half days. Their service from Austin to San Antonio had stops in San Marcos, Bonito, Guadalupe City, New Braunfels, and Cibolo (later called Selma). Headquarters for them in Austin were at the SWISHER Hotel on 6th and Congress. In June 1849, a second route was added leaving Austin and San Antonio every Monday and Friday at 6:00 a.m. and arriving at the other terminal at 6:00 p.m. The stages never ran on Sunday, but when one left Austin and one left San Antonio, they passed each other in Stringtown at the lower end of Hays County. There was a hotel there operated by William MOON, and it became well known. The route went to the foot of Congress, was transported by an old ferry boat across the river, crossed Williamson Creek, Slaughter Creek, went two miles farther across Onion Creek and one mile later was in Manchaco Springs. Col. John WEIR had the stage stop there with stables and the necessary equipment. So that shows they had the Texas U.S. Mail line between San Antonio and Houston, the Western U.S. Mail line between San Antonio and Port Lavaca, and the stage line between San Antonio and Corpus Christi.

The names of the stage stops have mostly been forgotten unless a community was able to build around the commerce. Bastrop, for instance, had a cypress and cedar house to use for stage exchanges, and it became well known. Sam HOUSTON stopped there several times in his trips to Austin. But there were places like Cane Island and Hog Eye (first named Young's Settlement) that couldn't match the growth of the plantation economy of La Grange or Jacksonville. Irish Creek settlement, later known as BURNS Station, was a stop from Victoria to Gonzales.

A bill was filed with the government for payment of carrying mail in 1847, but it was not paid until 1850.

> Post Master General, he is hereby directed to allow and pay to BROWN and TARBOX from the revenues of the Post Office appropriated for mail transportation the

sum of eight hundred dollars and eighty-four cents for temporary mail service on route number six thousand one hundred forty-nine in the state of Texas from the first day of July to the twenty-third day of October in the year 1847.
   Approved May 6, 1850

The faster "Mud" wagons were half the price of the big Concord Butterfield stages (which might cost $1600) and more wagon than coach. The majority of them were built by two wheelwrights, J.S. ABBOT and Lewis DOWNEY, in their New Hampshire factory. They could carry as few as four and as many as twelve people, but they were so much cheaper than the Concords that early stage coach owners had to use them. They were designed for speed with no doors. Passengers were expected to climb in over the sides. Three boards were placed across the body, and that was the perch. Wheels were smaller, wider, farther apart with a body that didn't swing side to side but moved forward and back. They were so uncomfortable that advertisements in later trips would say, "No Mud Wagons Used." With canvas sides and a roof, it was not the leisurely ride that television shows and movies present. The ride was dusty, hot or cold depending on the time of year, with no way to sleep or doze. Leaning on another passenger was frowned upon. A *San Antonio Herald* reporter wrote, "To make excellent jam, squeeze six or eight women now-a-days into a common stagecoach."

The classic 1939 Hollywood movie *Stagecoach* with John WAYNE showed six passengers, a conductor, and a driver in a beautiful Concord coach with three pairs of well-groomed horses. With ample room for legs, the stops showed traveling in leisure. In reality, a mud wagon would have mail and passengers squeezed together with knees touching, baggage on top, mail stacked everywhere, shocking dust in the hot weather and intense cold in the winter, and a hard journey. The movie's themes of redemption, community, society, social class, and the emphasis to overcome obstacles would have been lost on a passenger of 1848 who only wanted to get to a destination before his or her body suffered too much.

Drivers were expected to hitch a new team in no more than ten minutes when they came to a stage stop. The distance between stops could vary from twelve to fifteen miles apart. BROWN and TARBOX in an earlier ad in 1847 told of what the passengers could observe as they rode.

> The connecting line of stages is arranged as to pass through the principal forms and over the most valuable portion of Western Texas, a portion of country not surpassed by any in the United States, taking into consideration the advantages of climate, good water, and fertility of soil. This line is run by Four Horse carriages throughout; the carriages have been manufactured in Texas especially for mail transportation and are the only

carriages that can be successfully used at the present state of the roads."

They believed their drivers were the best that could be employed. "Our drivers are careful and skilled...punctual responsible ones...have interest directly in the route." Drivers were usually under forty and had good driving skills as well as courage to avoid robbers and Indians. The reins were called ribbons, and a driver used his left hand to hold them and his right hand for a brake. On some routes, a driver would have a particular section that he drove over and over because it was his favorite, and he would be fiercely protective of it. When a driver carried mail, he had to swear the "Oath of Mail Contractors and Carriers" and abide by its rules. Usually a driver's outfit was a long linen duster with long gloves. He wore a wide-brimmed hat, tall boots, and carried a whip. That was the reason a driver was often called "Whip" by the riders. Other generic names for the driver were "Jehu" or "Charlie." If a coach could not be safely handled, then express riders were substitutes. Another of their lines came from Indianola to handle small packages and freight as well as mail service since immigrants from Germany were beginning to pour into the Hill Country from Germany.

But agents for the stage lines and drivers had to deal with the same problems that all Texans did, illness and poor water. The obituary for an agent and a driver shows in 1849 the troubles everyone faced. "Mr. OSBURN of this city (Austin) who was engaged as an agent of Messrs. BROWN and TARBOX lately died at or near Austin, and Mr. CHAPMAN, one of the stage drivers, also died on the road to Bexar of a disease resembling cholera. The passengers have arrived from the west and report that several cases of the cholera have occurred at Austin, Bexar, Independence, and New Braunfels, and the disease is remarkably virulent."

Agents and station stop managers had a book with a map of their route, time tables, and room for any notes for drivers to make if it was necessary about the mail or cargo. Mail might be stuffed inside amidst the riders, and when the stage was full, at least eight people could sit inside with others riding on top. The mail was the most important part of the stage, and the U.S. mail contracts required that the line move at least fifteen miles a day regardless of the weather or condition of the road. It was that contract that kept the line in business. Some spoke of impassable roads, irresponsible carriers, and indifferent post markers, but the mail was delivered as it had not been before.

Average speed for the mud wagons was about five miles an hour, and the dust kicked up by the team and coach covered those inside. It was an exhausting experience and a meal at any stage stop was not known to be good. It could be bread, jerky, bad coffee, and beans—most assuredly beans. Cost for a meal might begin at forty cents and go higher if a more lavish spread were available. A twenty-four-hour ride might have three meals on average, but they were meant to be quick. A New York Herald correspondent Waterman L. ORMSBY wrote, "The fair, though rough, is better than could be expected so far from civilized districts. It consists of bread, tea, and fried steaks of bacon, venison, antelope or mule flesh—the latter tough."

Stage stops ranged in every size imaginable. The Fanthrop Inn in Washington-on-the-Brazos was a single dogtrot cabin with additions added much later. The Chappell Hill in Brenham was considered elegant by those standards. Stockton's Inn in Evergreen was also a pleasant station. An average time between stops was four hours. Owners of the stage probably added four-horse teams as soon as possible to make it faster.

There were no assigned seats, so riders hated to make a move at a stop if they had settled in a particularly good spot. A $20 ticket would be equal to more than $500 today, so occupants took their tickets seriously even when they felt every jolt. Major David TWIGGS tried to ride a stage coach from Houston to Austin on the TARBOX – BROWN line to get to his headquarters in Austin. But the coach bogged down twenty-five miles from Houston because of recent heavy rains, and it was impossible to go any farther. He turned around and rode back to Houston. He later went back to New Orleans, took a ship to Galveston, and went overland from there.

When the BROWN – TARBOX stage line reached San Antonio and fulfilled Mail Route #6152, its headquarters were leased from VANCE and BROTHERS in the city with a back room, livery stable, and spare lot. It was all that was necessary to keep the mail going. Stops in town might have included the Central Hotel, Navarro House, Plaza House, or Veramendi House with its big stables at the back.

The danger with robbers and Indians still existed. One stage owner gave up on his plans to own a prosperous line through no fault of his own. He said just that in a newspaper:

> The line of stages between this place and San Antonio has been discontinued in consequence of the impossibility of keeping relays of horses on the route, over twenty animals having been stolen from the proprietors by the Indians.

The Gonzales to San Antonio Road was busy once more. It was a way to make money for BROWN and TARBOX, but there was certainly competition.

Other stage companies such as HARRISON and MCCULLOUGH made sure to compete with times and locations. In October 1847, Thomas COOPER began a stage line from Lavaca to San Antonio by way of Victoria, Cuero, Gonzales,

Seguin, and finally San Antonio. The five-day trip cost $20. Also, a freight line ran every two weeks from Corpus Christi to San Antonio at $1 per one hundred pounds.

HARRISON and MCCULLOUGH began their line in Victoria and extended it to New Braunfels by way of Cuero and Gonzales. A passenger would leave Friday at 6:00 a.m. and arrive in New Braunfels at 4:00 p.m. Monday paying $10 for the trip. One crossing on the Cibolo was called BROWN's by all those who came to the county, and many who were first timers referred to him as "LIMPY." Since it had belonged to LOCKHART some years earlier, he must have bought it from LOCKHART's estate. Perhaps he thought that crossing deserved special attention as a mail stop to keep the route moving, but in 1849, he sold the stage stop to Georgia-born Thomas J. PERRYMAN (see Ch. 3), and according to early reports he moved a few miles up the Cibolo.

Below this stage stop was the sprawling Carvajal Ranch. Buying the stage stop from BROWN was just another business move that PERRYMAN felt had potential. He was known for his fine Waggoner race horse and for being able to manage so many parts of his life.

Financial claims came often against BROWN and TARBOX because of the system that spread out over Texas. One was for $331.91 on a debt that a business claim was owed to them. But they were not afraid to advertise for their postal and stage lines. One said that those coming from Indianola could ship "small packages in express boxes for fifty cents."

On a personal matter, TARBOX took out an ad in the *Houston Democratic* and *Texas Register* papers to say that he had lost a certificate for 120 acres in Harris County and hoped someone would find it and return it to him before he had to pay for a copy.

By 1850, the major players were established in their locations. TARBOX had married Jane CARROLL probably in 1845 or 1846 in Texas, and they had a daughter, Gertrude. The census shows them living with another family who may or may not be relatives. It is headed by Elizabeth Brown HADEN SMITH, wife of James W. SMITH. Her daughter Caroline has married Sydney BROWN. Is there a connection to John B.? None that can be shown.

1850 CENSUS, TRAVIS COUNTY, TEXAS #229

SMITH, Elizabeth	38	no occupation given
BROWN, SYDNEY	30	
TARBOX, Lyman	37	stage contractor $10,000 Personal value
Jane	22	
Gertrude	3	

BROWN was some distance away in Eagle

Pass on the Rio Grande. Perhaps he was acquiring more stock for their partnership. It is still listed as a part of Bexar County. His Irish-born wife, the former Margaret LOWRY, is beginning to see that BROWN will move often.

1850 CENSUS, BEXAR COUNTY, TEXAS
#17

BROWN, John—33—stock buyer--$8,000 personal value
Margaret—27
Charles—8
Margaret—7
Elisabeth—5
Frances—3
George—4 1/2

Clairborne RECTOR is on Cibolo Creek and the Ecleto with three children.

PERRYMAN had settled into his ranching in the Lower Cibolo Valley and doing well.

Spring of 1850 brought the announcement of a luxurious coach to the BROWN and TARBOX line. This was not done in their usual style of ordinary, but quick, wagons. The reporter almost gushed over what they had done.

> BROWN and TARBOX have completed another of their superior coaches for the Houston and San Antonio lines. It is Christened the "General Taylor." Its running gear is strong ash, the body and panels are of magnolia; its leather springs and its axles were forged in their own shop; the

boxes were cast and polished at MCGOWAN's furnace.

Thus, from the top tire to the top railing, from boat to pole, it is nothing else but Texas and Texan workmanship. The painting is done in a tasteful manner. The panels are ornamented with a spread eagle, bearing in his beak, a scroll, on which appears the name of the coach. The four wheels have a larger diameter than usual. The body is long, narrow and trim, giving ample room for three rows of passengers.

There is no later notice of what happened to the *General Taylor* although a similar ornate coach that was said to be named *General Sam Houston* was parked at the side of a stable in Austin until a city ordinance in 1907 said all alleys had to be cleared. It had been allowed to deteriorate until there was no way to move it, so all parts of it were destroyed and the timber was torn to pieces.

Compliments in 1850 came from some areas such as the *San Antonio Western Texan* newspaper. "There has been one route where there has not been a single failure! —WE speak of this route between this place and Houston. Messrs. BROWN and TARBOX have been as faithful as could possibly be required. They have made almost superhuman exertions in order to fulfill their contracts."

Another glowing account was printed by the *Houston Telegraph* which gave the stagecoach line high praise.

The contractors Messrs. BROWN and TARBOX have

performed the work assigned to them in a manner highly creditable to themselves and satisfaction to the people along the whole line of the venture. When the prairies were soft, their carriages bogged down. They had a new wheel made with broad tires which could stand on the turf when other wheels would mire up to the hubs. We commend these energetic and public-spirited contractors to the favorable notice of the department at Washington.

Even the government got into the company's business as the lawmakers in Austin asked for more money for the job BROWN and TARBOX had been doing on February 11, 1850.

Joint Resolution for the Relief of Brown and Tarbox

Whereas LYMAN TARBOX and J.F. BROWN, mail contractors on route No.__; and whereas the said BROWN and TARBOX conveyed said mail each alternate day during the last session of the legislature, when they were only bound to carry the same service weekly, thereby greatly facilitating the transmission of intelligence to land from the capitol of said state of Texas; therefore

Be it resolved by the Legislature of the state of Texas that our senators and representatives in the United States Congress are instructed to urge the passage of a law for the relief of said BROWN and TARBOX by compensating them for said extra services. Feb. 11, 1850.

So, the business was going well—or so it seemed. But in late 1850 BROWN and TARBOX dissolved the stage lines to concentrate on the mail delivery. Maintaining and providing for a stage line was incredibly expensive. Competition from more than twenty-five other lines including HARRISON and MCCULLOUGH was fierce. PERRYMAN and RECTOR kept their stops for mail delivery. It was an effort to cut down on the cost of maintaining all that went with the stages. A bid in May 1850 for a new postal service, Star Route 6285, between Austin and San Antonio went to another group, HARRISON and MCCULLOUGH for almost $2,900. Four other stage lines had bids on the route: BROWN and TARBOX, CAPSHAW and GRANT, L. SIMS and BROTHERS, and Levi SHACKLEFORD. So that meant BROWN and TARBOX lost a $3,000 contract. Even HARRISON and MCCULLOUGH would have tough times and get out of the stage and freighting business within the next few years. By 1861, the major lines would be under the control of SAWYER and RISHER.

A stage stop at Cibolo, later called Selma, between Austin and San Antonio, had been built in the previous years and used almost daily though not for overnight stays. At first it was probably a one room log cabin, but eventually, it became something for the ten to twelve horses that needed to be ready for exchange and for the men who tended them. Walls were made of lime, sand, pebbles, and corn cobs. It was an early form of concrete known as "tabby" and was a place to change teams but not to eat or sleep. It was about 576 sq. feet with cedar shingles.

The Selma Stage Stop was not big but important as the stages made their way from one point to another. With more than a dozen lines striving to get the best jobs, it was more difficult as each day went by. Most lines had to have as many as 300 drivers as well as 1,000 horses and mules.

Sometime in 1850, TARBOX and wife, Jane, took a trip to Tennessee after the death of Phillip CALLAGHAN in Davison County. The connection seems to be from CALLAGHAN's first wife, Maria CARROLL, who would likely have been Jane's close relative. Family records report that Maria came from Dublin, but the Tennessee roots are evident in later family members such as Jane. A lawsuit filed by the executor of Phillip's estate asked the court to arrest Lyman and Jane TARBOX and to retrieve two slaves and some other personal property belonging to the estate. The petitioner states that Phillip CALLAGHAN's personal property included two slaves (ten-year-old John and six-year-old Chesterfield), "a mantle timepiece of the value of $50, a feather bed worth $20, and a portrait of the testator's first wife worth $50.

He reports that "within the last twenty-four hours the two have seduced from the care & possession of the agent in whose keeping your orator had placed them the two negroes...that between the hours of ten and twelve today they went to a back door into the house of the agent and fraudulently and furtively carried off said clock, feather bed, and portrait." He also states that the TARBOXES "are of low means and irresponsible for any damages in their torts or contracts" and are planning to "flee back to their home state of Texas."

Michael CALLAGHAN says he will incur great expense pursuing them and will not recover the value of the property because of the defendants' poverty. He asks the court to arrest the TARBOXES and retrieve the estate property holding them until the case is tried. So much for great family relationships, and the TARBOXES came back to Texas probably with the clock, feather bed and portrait but not both slaves. This is evident by another filing by CALLAGHAN in 1851 when he asks the court for a judgment so that he can sell the slave John in order to pay a specific legacy to Ellen CALLAGHAN, daughter of the deceased Phillip. He states in the petition that there were three slaves left at the death of Phillip and four minor children—no mention of the property which he says was taken by going through his back door.

But in 1851 an even more abrupt change took place: TARBOX sold his half of the partnership to BROWN. The announcement was put in the Houston paper to show things were over between the two. It announced that the change in the partnership had been made March 10 but was not in the paper until August 25.

The co-partnership heretofore existing under the

name of BROWN and TARBOX has been dissolved. The undersigned having purchased the interest of Lyman TARBOX in the same, the business will hereafter be conducted by him on his own account. Thankful for the very liberal patronage heretofore extended, he will use every endeavor to merit its continuance. He respectfully solicits a continuance of the public Patronage

J.F. BROWN

An announcement was also seen in the *Washington on the Brazos* paper on July 5.

The firm of BROWN and TARBOX is this day dissolved by mutual consent. All those indebted to said firm will make payments to J.F. BROWN. He will also pay debts due by said firm. Having purchased the entire interest of Lyman TARBOX, I will continue to run an accommodation line from Houston to Austin.

J.F. BROWN

An announcement in the Galveston paper was similar but added more details.

NOTICE—the partnership heretofore existing under The name and style of BROWN and TARBOX was dissolved on the 20th of March last. The staging business will hereafter be carried on By J.F. BROWN who has purchased the interest of LYMAN TARBOX and by mutual arrangement, he alone, is authorized to settle the outstanding business of the firm. On and after the 20th of the preset month, the present schedule will be changed, so as to run through from Houston to Austin in two days starting as is present every other day.

The undersigned respectfully solicits a continuance of the patronage which has been so liberally extended to him during the past ten years.

J.F. BROWN

So, BROWN says that he has been in the business of stages and/or hotels since 1841.

As a horseman, maybe TARBOX wanted to do something else. Earlier, he had joined with John J. GRUMBLES to establish a ferry, one that would benefit the people of Austin. The action was cited in the minutes of the Speaker of the Texas House on January 7, 1850.

Petition from citizens of Travis County for the Legislature to pass law authorizing TARBOX and John J. GRUMBLES both citizens of Travis County to establish a ferry on the Colorado River, opposite the city of Austin, free of charge to citizens of Austin.

GRUMBLES, a former Texas Ranger, and well-known figure, had bought and sold land on the Colorado. But something happened to keep the two from continuing with their plans. On May 26, 1851, there is a listing in Travis County Deeds for John J. GRUMBLES to Jenny M. TARBOX for $150, lots 8 and 9 in Block 54. Jenny is Lyman's wife shown as "Jane" in the 1850 census. There is another parcel of land sold to GRUMBLES on May 3. And by the next year, 1852, GRUMBLES is advertising a ferry that is not a free one.

CITY FERRY

A large and new boat of superior construction and finish, sixty-seven feet long by twelve feet wide, and capable of crossing in entire safety a wagon and team of six yoke of oxen. The banks are in good condition, and no detention in crossing need be apprehended in day time or night.

RATES

Wagon loaded and six yoke oxen – $1.00
Carriage and one horse –.20
Man horse –.10

Lyman is not mentioned in the land transaction or the ferry. Perhaps he realized there would be other ferry operations with a great deal of competition. Or, he might have seen some of the physical problems that would have to be addressed as a later ad stated that citizens "must not bathe in the Colorado River or in the vicinity of GRUMBLES Ferry. A fine of $10 will be assessed." It was said to be against the peace and quiet of the community.

He had trained a bay horse that had been part of an estate sale. In an advertisement for a Livery Stable on Pecan Street in September 1851, the owner notes that Lyman TARBOX will be in charge of the stable. Other ads in December, then April, May, June, July, August, and September 1852 continue to show TARBOX as the person who will handle the stable duties. Oddly enough, TARBOX never seemed to pay taxes on any property in Travis County after that time although he had paid them in Harris County in 1847, 1848, and 1849. Two more parcels of land are sold by Lyman and his wife to Euclid EARNEST in Travis County on May 21, 1853.

BROWN kept the daily line from Austin to Houston for a short time and also orchestrated the line from Washington on the Brazos to Houston, an ad in the summer of 1851 reported the activity.

> Daily Line of coaches from Washington to Houston the accommodating line of stages hereafter make their trip daily from Washington to Houston and from Houston to Washington.
> TRI-WEEKLY
> The coaches shall at all times be the best the condition of the roads will allow.
> J.F. BROWN

Where would the stage stops have been? Certainly, it would have depended on the roads which were barely more than a network of trails where one path branched off from another one at points. Washington on the Brazos was a frequent steamboat stop and export destination for cotton with service industries and commerce. It would have stage stops that catered to travelers. Places like Hempstead, Waller, Hockley, and Cypress could all have been stopping points. But he found it too difficult for the operation without his partner. He then sold what was left of BROWN and TARBOX to other lines and continued to buy and sell livestock.

Loans had been taken out and perhaps not repaid. In 1851 in Washington County, a James LAWSON filed suit against BROWN and TARBOX for three notes he believed had not been settled. The amount was approximately $579.06. He speaks of BROWN by saying, "The defendant JOHN F. BROWN is a transient person and so secrets himself that the ordinary process of the law cannot be served upon him." Although the initial is different from the "John B.," it is the former stage coach owner. "Goods, wares, and merchandise we sold and delivered to them and cash advanced," was stated by LAWSON. No mention is made of TARBOX. So, is BROWN moving so much that the law cannot catch up with him? Or is it just the manner of making money quickly by the buying and selling of land in Texas.

It is not easy to keep track of BROWN and TARBOX after they have sold their interests in stage lines. A person named John B. BROWN bought 640 acres on Wallace's Creek which has some origin in Comal County. By 1850, BROWN and his family had moved to Eagle Pass on the Rio Grande. At first it had been a trading post but became more important with the building of Fort Duncan two miles upstream. When BROWN came to Eagle Pass, there had been a flurry of activity for transporting goods, and he helped to lay plans to develop a stage line as well as a freight line. It was difficult in the planning because Eagle Pass was a distance from San Antonio without much settlement in between. Also, the area was known as a haven for outlaws and slave hunters; the danger was always present for permanent residents. About 1851, BROWN took his family back to Comal County.

Between 1851 and 1858, BROWN became partners with lawyer William DAVENPORT who had moved south of Cibolo Creek on what had been part of the Vicente MICHELI survey, and the two ran cattle and horses on the open range. They branded the horses and other livestock with their distinctive brands, a WD for DAVENPORT and BROWN's big "Diamond B" which he had used for many years. "Captain DAVENPORT had an easy relationship with the Lipan Apache who were across the Cibolo from him and was impressed by the clay ovens they used to bake sotol.

In 1853, however, his neighbors suffered the loss of a young son. It was described by another rancher in this way. "The poor little fellow was riding a mule and had no chance to escape from the savages. He was the first to discover them and called out to his companion who was in advance, to 'look there what ugly men' were coming. He was soon roped and dragged to the ground, fearfully tortured and finally killed and scalped."

An uneasy peace lasted only a short time. Settlers watched for any signs of Indians on their property. At least a dozen horses were taken from around the Seguin area, and another man was killed in 1854. In 1855 other Indians, probably a blend of Kickapoo, Tonkawa, and Comanche stole horses up and down the Cibolo. So, a plan was set to catch them in the act of horse stealing; it did not work, and a letter was sent to the Governor to ask for help.

GOV'R PEASE   24 SEPT. '55

A party of Indians on Friday night last drove off from the Cibolo near the crossing of the stage road sixty horses of which forty-nine belonged to Mr. DAVENPORT.

It seems that the Indians were known to have been in the neighborhood, and a party had been searching for them.

On Friday night their horses were driven out onto the prairie with the intention of watching them and detecting them in the act of taking them. Some mistake occurred about the meeting of the party, and the Indians carried off the horses.

The stage driver says the horses were driven away while the men were at supper.

On September 20th, then, the plan to catch the Indians in the act of stealing horses had not worked, so DAVENPORT got nine men to go with him to trail the bandits. They stayed after the Indians for nine days until they came upon them in the Medina Valley. It had been very rough going, but they were determined to get the horses back and make an example of the Indians. The groups met. All the Indians were killed, and the chief was scalped. His scalp and shield were taken to the father of the boy who was killed two years earlier. It was said the father carried them around for years and showed them to others.

After being in Eagle Pass for ten years, BROWN set down roots in Comal County and acquired more land there. He was living in the Davenport area (later Bracken) with Christian BUSCH as his neighbor. Communication between BROWN and his neighbors must have been an interesting set of dialects as BROWN surely had a Scottish or Irish brogue while all of the immigrants around him were from Germany and spoke only German or spoke English with a strong German accent. His personal wealth is lower, but it is possible that his place was a stage stop. He knew the value of having such a location for whoever ran the stage lines. It had been too much for him as sole owner, but he could make money by having a place for the stage to change horses. His taxes in Comal County began in 1852 and continued for almost twenty years.

A certain John BROWN bought the PATTON tract on Cibolo Creek on March 11, 1852. There is a letter in the Gonzales Post Office in 1853 which he never picked up. In 1856, he is named as an appraiser for the estate of John D. GROESBECK, a wagon maker, in Bexar County and perhaps someone who had done work for the stage line.

1860 CENSUS, COMAL COUNTY

BROWN, John B.—49—farmer—real estate value $6000 personal $1550

    Margaret—37
    Charles—18
    Margaret—16
    Elisabeth—13
    Frances—10
    George—9
    Louisa—6
    Jasper—5

He has one laborer who is helping on the farm or stage stop. There is the possibility that the oldest son in the family, Charles, was part of the Texas participation in the Civil War. There are five Charles BROWNs who are listed as veterans, but there is no way to know if he died in the war. He is not listed with the family in the 1870 census.

The Gonzales to Guadalupe Road continued to be used during the Civil War with movement of supplies for troops or soldiers going to a different assignment. But it was clear that with the coming of the railroad, the old lines would be redrawn, and the road would have seen its importance diminish.

In another ten years the family is still in Comal County and with declining fortune as were many residents of the area after the Civil War.

1870 CENSUS, COMAL COUNTY

BROWN, John—56—farmer—real estate value $3420
    Personal $1120
    Margaret—48
    Elisabeth—20
    Frances—19
    George—16
    Louisa—14
    Josephine—9
    William—36

The "William BROWN" listed at the end of the census for the family is the slave who was with them in 1850. He took their last name and was now listed as a domestic servant. He cannot read or write. For the rest of his life, he will work for John B. or one of the children and be counted with them as they move around Texas.

A move to Bexar County came about 1871 and BROWN continued on the tax rolls there for more than twenty years. The idea of being a hotel manager again must never have left BROWN's mind. He sold his land in Comal and built a hotel in Bexar County outside San Antonio. In Victoria, his hotel had been called BROWN's. The name for his new place connected to his Scottish roots when he called it Highland Home. If it was built sometime after the 1870 census, it could have been a stage stop for the stages coming out of San Antonio. The stagecoach business would be able to hold on for another ten years, and Highland Home would have been in a perfect spot for the first stop west out of San Antonio going toward El Paso and San Diego. That stage route was a very busy one after the Civil War.

1880 CENSUS, BEXAR COUNTY

BROWN, John—65—hotel manager
Margaret—55
Elisabeth—27
Josephine—16
DURST, Francis—25
John—3

Where was Highland Home? It was described as west of San Antonio. An early-day settler of the community of Somerset mentioned that among the first people who had land there was a Mr. BROWN, a stock raiser from Scotland." That certainly fits. It would not have been built in the county where few people would take advantage of the rooms, so the idea of a stage stop would be enticing. Another entry said a "John BROWN worked on the Joshua Crossing of the Boerne Road." And this is where the clues lead us to the location.

In 1855, Max AUE built a half-story limestone rubble saltbox house in the area called Leon Springs a few miles from Boerne. His place became a stage stop from San Antonio to Bandera and Fredericksburg, a route that ran three times a week for the cost of $4.75 to take the eleven-hour trip.

It also became the first stop on the San Antonio to San Diego Mail Route, No. 8067. It had its dangers because of the Leon and Huebner Creeks which ran full most of the time. But the area northwest of San Antonio was considered prime land, and this is most likely where BROWN built his new hotel about 1871.

AUE's stage stop was the primary one, but more than one line came through Leon Springs, so there was room for another place. There was a population of at least fifty, a general store, a steam cotton gin, and a post office, so the future looked promising as BROWN continued to buy and sell land and livestock. He paid taxes in Bexar County from 1872 through 1895. He and AUE competed for the passengers who came through the area on their way to far-off places, and the rivalry was productive for both owners.

Threats of Indian attacks had ended, but robbers still saw the isolated locations as prime targets. One group came to Leon Springs in the 1870's and robbed AUE's store, which was at the bottom of his stage stop building. They tied up AUE and his family, took food, horses, supplies, and clothes before leaving. AUE's reputation as a hunter and tracker was well known. However, the bandits were not counting on his determination to find them. AUE got free, rode to Boerne, organized a posse, tracked, and killed the culprits. Before the last man died, he called out, "Tell the old man I'm wearing his clothes."

All was not a peaceful happy ending for BROWN. A fire ripped through Highland Home in January 1881. Since it was eight miles west or more to San Antonio, little help could be directed to putting out the blaze. Value was set at $5000. The family and boarders escaped with their lives but nothing else. There was a $2000 insurance policy to help with the accident.

> About 1:30 o'clock last night, Highland Home was entirely destroyed by fire. Nothing whatever was saved. The property was owned by J.B. BROWN, known as Limpy. The fire originated in the kitchen and when it was discovered, the whole building was in flames. Several of the family and boarders barely escaped with their lives. Mrs. BROWN escaped without her clothing. Her husband lost $548 in currency and a boarder lost $300 and other smaller amounts. The family and boarders took shelter with neighbors temporarily.

The years ahead were active in some ways as newspapers reported that BROWN stayed at the Menger Hotel in San Antonio, attended a bank opening in Fort Worth, and was also in Galveston. In 1883, BROWN attended a veterans' reunion and his address was given as Highland Home. Perhaps he had rebuilt the structure. From later mentions it seems clear he had. He paid his dues to the Texas Veterans Association at least through 1886. In 1885, his daughter Elisabeth was at a gathering, and her address was shown as Highland Home. He and his family would have been traveling by train since a line had been completed to San Antonio in 1877. Stagecoaches were becoming a thing of the past. The GONZALES to SAN ANTONIO Road and all its spinoffs had lost purpose for travelers. The railroad companies touted the success of their ventures with big ads.

GALVESTON, HARRISBURG,
AND SAN ANTONIO RAILWAY
This is the direct line to all parts
NORTH, EAST, and SOUTHEAST
Through Palace Sleeping Coaches
From San Antonio to New Orleans without change.
The Shortest and Most Direct Routes To Eastern Cities.

In 1890 and 1892, BROWN filed claims for India depredation against him and waited to see if he would receive some kind of compensation. A question of his citizenship was in the argument. A year before in 1889 his wife, Margaret, had died, so his world became a different place. But before he could receive a judgment on his claim, BROWN died at Highland Home on January 29, 1897. It would be 1917 before the claims reached the federal level, and the Senate and House of Representatives Court of Claims ruled "without reference to the citizenship of John B. BROWN now deceased" with a later statement stating he was "assured to be a U.S.

citizen at the time of claims."

John B. "Limpy" BROWN and his wife Margaret were buried in the Alamo Masonic Cemetery in San Antonio. The man born in Glasgow had been a Texan for most of his life and would remain there.

But perhaps even more perplexing is the disappearance of Lyman TARBOX from any census or newspaper or record. In 1850, TARBOX sells land to James F. JOHNS. In 1841 he had sold land to James F. BROWN in Travis County (is that our John B. or a completely different person?) His wife JENNY sells a parcel of land on May 22, 1851 to Henry PFLEGERAND in Travis County. He has a few ventures in Austin that seem rather simple, and then there is quiet until 1856 when a single letter comes as a reprint to the *Central Texas* (Anderson) paper from the Houston paper. TARBOX says he had gone to Iowa for a year and disliked the weather. But rather than return to Texas and have money to show for it, he had joined the expedition to Nicaragua headed by William WALKER. This venture was widely hailed by some in southern states but ignored by the federal government because WALKER had decided on his own to become the new president of the small country and extend the slave territory. TARBOX sounds as though he has fallen under the spell of WALKER who took volunteers and managed to gain control for a short period. The letter shows that those who believed in

WALKER saw his attempts to take a territory as the right experience. The letter says:

Granada 1856

You may be surprised when you see from whence this is dated. The climate of Iowa was too cold for a southerner, therefore, 6th of April we started for this country. After living in Council Bluffs for one year, I found it was no country for a Texian. Too proud to return to Texas as poor as when we left it, we came out here.

Our country is far ahead of Texas in everything. All kinds of employment are amply repaid by the government. I am Wagon-Master-General of the State and get $150 a month and rations. A soldier gets $25 a month and rations, and $25 for clothes every six months. A captain gets $100 and all kinds of mechanics are well paid.

All kinds of fruit can be grown here: orange, lemon, pineapple, coconut, vanilla bean, bananas, plantains, figs, and in Costa Rica the finest peaches and apples. The sugar here is far superior to the Texas sugar. They also raise rice, tobacco, indigo, cotton, and corn, of which last, three crops a year are harvested.

Billy Walker is bound to succeed. He has the confidence of the people and that is all that is necessary.

There is a fine chance of staging from Virgin Bay to San Juan del Sur on the Pacific Coast, a distance of 12 miles. All the California travel goes that way now and from here to Leon, 100 miles, over a prettiest level country you ever saw though there is no communication now because of the war.

TARBOX sees the trek to Nicaragua as

a great chance to make a new life and sees the country as a virtual paradise, "far ahead of Texas in everything." He might have gone to California to sign up as a goodly number of men who went with WALKER were from there. But there were also other places that heard of WALKER and flocked to be one of his band.

William WALKER would have an adventurous but doomed experience. Although only five-feet-two with a slender frame and thinning hair, WALKER was so charismatic that he was said to have people believing in his ideas from the first words he spoke. With a medical degree and a legal degree, he could have practiced medicine and law (and did for short spells) but decided in 1853 to establish a republic out of the lower portion of California and the upper portion of Mexico. Those who believed in this action were called "filibusters," not for speaking for long periods of time, but because they wanted to expand the United States into new areas. His first recruiting office was in San Francisco where volunteers came from everywhere to join with him.

At least two different attempts to establish new territories saw fierce fighting and loss of lives, and each time he was brought back to the United States and tried on the charge of violating neutrality rules. However, no prosecution was a match for him, and he was found not guilty each time. On May 4, 1855, he and another group of volunteers who called themselves "The IMMORTALS" headed for Nicaragua. This would fit into the time that TARBOX wrote his letter back to Houston. Once again, WALKER was taken into custody by the United States authorities and returned for a trial in New Orleans—which he won.

There is no way to know if TARBOX stayed with WALKER after the 1856 tour. WALKER left the confusion and fighting in May 1857 to return to the United States but returned in November. Some had stayed with him since the beginning; some deserted his cause. Because of disorganization and failure to win over the natives of the area, WALKER's followers could see no hope for continuing.

WALKER's luck could not hold out forever, so a fourth attempt to become the president of a new country (which was really the old country of Honduras) failed as revolutionists defeated him and his men. He was executed with only twelve men left to tell the story.

Historically, the ventures were a colossal mistake and cost hundreds of men their lives. Did TARBOX die in any of the action? Did he suffer from the outbreaks of cholera that killed many of the volunteers? Did he escape to Costa Rica or Panama? Did he return to the United States? He would have been at least forty-three years old with little money, and his successful partnership was a distant memory. There is nothing to tell us of his whereabouts or if he went to a new place.

Another surprising mention of TARBOX

came in the Texas Supreme Court in 1863 in the case of CHAMBLEE vs. TARBOX. The question being decided by the judge was "similarity of name is said to be some evidence of identity." In 1844 TARBOX had bought land after a sheriff's sale and shortly thereafter gave it to Jane CARROLL who was to be his wife. It was 1,077 acres and had been obtained at an extremely cheap price. The land had originally been advertised at $5 an acre but got no bidders, so it was sold at a sheriff's sale for almost nothing. Then TARBOX bought it for another low price from that owner this time $500. Almost too good to be true, it would seem. The question to be argued: was Jane CARROLL the woman who became Jane TARBOX? The question seems easy enough, but the law had to proceed with a great deal of testimony and precedence to show that she was the heir to that land. There is no testimony by Lyman, but there is a Horace TARBOX who stands to defend Jane. Is that Lyman's brother? And does this prove that Lyman has died in Nicaragua?

Some of the pieces fall together when Horace's background is described. He was born in New York (as Lyman was) in Onondaga County in 1817. So, he would have been only a few years younger than Lyman. His parents were Peter TARBOX and Mary WOODRUFF TARBOX. In 1841, he left home and settled in Freeport, Illinois, where he established a hotel and livery business. In 1850 he went to Council Bluffs, Iowa, where he dealt with stock of every description. Lyman's letter of 1856 says that he went to live in Council Bluffs but didn't like the weather. The timing fits the exact time when Horace was living in the area. So, the two probable brothers both left the area. Horace went to Colorado, continued to buy, and sell land, moved back and forth between Colorado and Nebraska, Illinois, and eventually settled in Grand Island, Nebraska. His business knowledge would have been a great help to Jane as she faced the legal tangles of the land she thought she owned.

The case also hinged on whether Lyman and the sheriff had been in cahoots to get the land for such a low amount, and therefore it was fraud. A jury trial had come up with one decision, but the Supreme Court judge sent it back for another trial because there were so many jury instructions that were ignored. Was that the end of it? No, the precedent was used in similar cases in Maryland, North Carolina, the Philippines, and as late as 1944 in Strickland vs. Humble Oil. It was used in scholarly discussions such as *A Treatise on the Law of Identification* by George Horos. It was in *The American Decisions: Cases of General Value and Authority* compiled by A.C. Freeman. So, the thing that TARBOX's name has been used for more than a hundred years had nothing to do with his stagecoach or the crooked roads he challenged.

The Gonzales to San Antonio Road provided a way for military movement, immigrants, business travel, and postal deliveries. Thousands of wagons and horses and people had taken its course. Guadalupe County had become a more open place in its early days because of it. Changes in the modern world had swallowed the ruts behind private property and fences, so nothing could be seen of it in a matter of a few years. Stories of stage coaches and men like TARBOX and BROWN were left to the memories of the very few and then eventually forgotten. This was one of the few early roads in Texas that did not develop into something more permanent and important, and it, too, became a memory. What stories could be told about this road. What tales would describe the battles and experiences of those who came before there was anything to be seen on the Cibolo except its untamed strength?

TARBOX and BROWN left an influence on the area. There is a street in Buda, Texas, named after them.

CIVIL WAR

The question of secession from the Union was a hotbed of discussion. A choral society or "Sangerbund" in San Antonio in 1854 passed a resolution of disapproval of slavery. This caused a firestorm of disapproval from the settlers who were not German. Governor Sam HOUSTON was against anything that would take Texas out of the Union. When the vote came to make the local decision, less than half in Guadalupe County voted. It passed 314-22. Most German settlers believed in the Union and thought secession by the states was not lawful. They had connections to German relatives and friends in the North in places like Cincinnati and St. Louis and did not want to be part of action against them.

Some, however, had lived in the South long enough to feel they needed to support whatever was done by the state whatever their personal beliefs. The Banishment Act passed on August 8, 1861 stated all males over fourteen who considered themselves hostile to the Confederacy were to leave the state in forty days. It was a direct attack on any Germans who had been vocal in saying they could not support the Rebel side.

When the Conscription Act of 1862 passed, it stated males between the ages of eighteen and thirty-five were to serve in the Confederacy. Soon after, the age limit was broadened to forty-five. Wealthy citizens could hire substitutes for their sons. All male adults were to come to the county courthouse and sign a loyalty oath to the Confederacy.

German-born settlers had been passionate about the new democracy in Texas, established newspapers, gave parades on the Fourth of July, but they still spoke their German language and were distant from those who talked about states rights. They particularly disliked the Conscription Act because it reminded them of the laws they had left in their native Germany.

In December 1861, the Texas Legislature passed an act which stated all able-bodied men from eighteen to fifty with certain exceptions were to enroll for frontier defense, so male citizens were to either serve in the Confederacy or in companies that protected the Texas border against Indian raids. Those in Cibolo who farmed were often considered important for the War effort. Some could get exemptions as long as they provided goods.

Those who had the most land and were wealthiest at the start of the Civil War, German and Anglo alike, suffered losses during the War as the second figure represents their reported value five years later in 1870.

PERRYMAN	$25,000	$20,000
M. AMACHER	$ 3,000	$ 1,900
SNIDER	$ 1,400	no longer in county
JOHNSTON	$ 1,228	no longer in county
PFANNSTIEL	$ 1,272	still in county but no figure given
YEHL	$ 1,288	$ 700
ANDERSON	$ 1,050	$ 800
SEILER	$ 1,000	still in county but no figure given
BURBANK	$ 1,000	died in 1861
PFIEL	$ 900	$ 450

In 1863 PERRYMAN was indicted for placing ten African American slaves in charge of a farm with no free white person in charge of them. The custom was not unusual since some slaves had been with their owners since birth, but wartime made everyone more nervous about slaves who were on their own. He was fined $50 for his action.

It was a frightening time for all residents of the Valley during the Civil War as many German families in other Hill Country places farther west in communities such as COMFORT and KERRVILLE were taken out of their homes, beaten, murdered or lynched because they were suspected of being anti-Confederates. The number was said to be as high as twenty of those who were executed with more than that number imprisoned, both husbands and wives.

In July 1862, some Hill Country Germans

formed the Union Loyal League which was supposed to give support to the Union cause, and it was the source of violence for those who were known members. Approximately 500 men were actual members of the League's armed militia groups who decided who would live and die. Anyone who had not come in and signed the loyalty oath could be arrested as well as his family. One teenage boy and his grandfather of the TURKNETT family in another county were stopped, questioned about the boy's father who was suspected of being in the ULL, and when they would not give his whereabouts, they were beaten to death with a bullwhip.

August 1862 brought terror to all German families in Cibolo and the Hill Country. Sixty young men, mostly German but a few Anglo and one Mexican American, Pablo DIAZ, gathered south of KERRVILLE intending to travel to the west and the Mexican border. There they would join the Union Army and go to NEW ORLEANS or stay in MEXICO until it was safe to come home or make their way to California. But a series of mistakes in planning made them vulnerable to an attack by a group of Partisan Rangers, as they were called, and the trip ended with nineteen dead and at least eight or more wounded so severely they could not escape. The others scattered in the brushy landscape. The wounded were executed. An order was sent by the Ranger Commander, Captain James DUFF, that the bodies were to be left unburied. They remained where they had fallen until 1865, the end of the War, when their families gathered them and put the remains under a monument at COMFORT with the heading "Treue der Union," True to the Union. It would be the only German language monument to the Union in the south with a flag flown at half-staff from that date forward.

Although the Lower Valley of Cibolo was not a highly dangerous area, their neighboring counties were. Residents certainly knew what was happening and had friends or relatives who were involved in the imprisonments and killings. A few sent their sons to MEXICO or other cities to escape the threat of conscription. Some hid them in the fields whenever they saw a group of uniformed men heading to their homes. There were young men from the Valley, however, who served in the Confederate home troops without asking for special circumstances. They thought their families would be safe if they joined state forces which would not see much action.

Sometimes, they trained at Camp Clark near San Marcos or Camp Beauregard near Lake McQueeney. The Third Infantry was recruited in San Antonio and served along the Texas coast. They never saw any real action and disbanded before the 1865 surrender.

The First Regiment, Texas Mounted Rifles, was the first Texas regiment to be mustered into service and went on patrol in far West Texas to protect that part of the state from Indian attacks. Most brought their own horse, saddle, arms, and blankets, so if they were lost in a skirmish, it was a personal hardship.

In nearby Comal County, the citizens never tired of offering refreshment and music to those who had enlisted. A farewell dance was given in honor of Captain Theodore PODEWIL's Texas Mounted Riflemen in April 1862 before they went to train and then another dance in October 1862 when they completed training. For Captain BOS' Texas Volunteer Infantry, there was a dance in early 1862 and another in July of that same year. Training was done on the Colorado River about eight miles south of Austin.

Names appearing on the Confederate rolls are:

Carl CONRAD—7th Regiment, Texas Cavalry
John RITTIMAN—3rd Regiment, Confederate Infantry
William VORDENBAUM—1st Regiment, Texas Heavy Artillery
Otto BROTZ—8th Regiment, Texas Infantry
Fred BROTZ—7th Regiment, Texas Cavalry
George BERGFELD—3rd Regiment, Texas Infantry
Philip SCHRAUB—1st Field Battery, Texas Light Cavalry
August SHIMMELPFENNING—36th Regiment, Texas Cavalry
Henry GROBE—Texas Cavalry, Mounted Rifles
William STAPPER—3rd Regiment, Texas Infantry
Ferdinand DEITZ—8th Regiment, Texas Infantry
Gottlieb DEITZ—8th Regiment, Texas Infantry
August PFEIL—3rd Regiment, Texas Infantry

Heinrich WEIDNER—3rd Regiment, Texas Infantry
Louis SASSMANHAUSEN—36th Cavalry
Charley HILD—1st Regiment, Texas Cavalry
Ferdinand WEYEL—7th Regiment, Texas Cavalry
Adolph WEYEL—7th Regiment, Texas Cavalry
Carl FROMME—1st Regiment, Texas Heavy Artillery

At least two were mustered in on the Union side:
Melchoir BAEYER—1st Regiment, Texas Cavalry
Bernard BAEYER—1st Regiment, Texas Cavalry
Dr. Felix BRACHT was a field surgeon for the Confederacy in 5th Texas Cavalry.

All German homes were fiercely loyal to the Union but were careful of the statements they made around their neighbors. Newspapers talked of support for the Union, but the Cibolo farmers did not want to meet the fate of those who had been killed in other places. Tension was high because German-Americans did not want their friends and neighbors to think they would aid the Union. They farmed and gave provisions, particularly beef, to the Commissary Headquarters in San Antonio when a wagon was sent out.

Finally, in 1865 when the war ended, they could get back to the business of making a living on the Cibolo, but there would be hard feelings for years to come. Communities would never forget how they were treated.

Difficulties developed as soon as the war ended when a cholera epidemic hit San Antonio in

1866. Those who lived in Cibolo tried to avoid any contact with people who lived in the city as long as the problem existed. A new system for taking care of sanitation in the city was expected to solve the number of illnesses.

THE RAILROAD

1877—Change

Since 1850, plans had been ongoing to lay railroad tracks from Houston to other cities in Texas. The Bison Bayou, Brazos, and Colorado started the work but suffered money problems just as the Civil War hit and never recovered. A new name and ownership saw the Galveston, Harrisburg, and San Antonio Railway begin laying tracks. It was exciting for people in the Valley to think a train would connect them to San Antonio and other places around them.

The bad news came when the railroad announced its line: two miles from the Valley Post Office which was the only post office between New Braunfels, Seguin, and San Antonio. When a camp for railroad workers was built, it was also several miles north of the area where Valley action took place. This would later turn into the community of Marion and be a very busy depot for freight, one of the busiest in the state.

Valley butchers Edmund PFEIL and Otto

BROTZE supplied laborers in the railroad camps with meat while they built the railroad. One of eleven children born to Anton and Maria SCHMITZ PFEIL, Edmund, farmed in the Valley region. BROTZE was a stock herder and soon settled into farming and raising a family with wife Josephine PFEIL BROTZE. Work was slow as all building materials had to be hauled by open wagons from the end of the railroad line which was at that time centered in Kingsbury.

In February of 1877, the Galveston, Harrisburg, and San Antonio Railway announced that its line was complete into San Antonio, going through Seguin, HILDA (later called McQUEENEY), Marion CIBOLO VALLEY (the name for the depot), CUT OFF (later became SCHERTZ), and CONVERSE. It was a much better means of transportation for people and goods, but it may have made a difference if the location had been where the community wanted it to be.

Trains stopped in Cibolo if a passenger wished to travel to San Antonio, Seguin, or a nearby community. Since there was no passenger agent at this point, it was FROMME's job to flag down the train and make it stop. It was simple enough if the train was going toward San Antonio as it could be seen easily enough from the east. But it was a different story if the train headed for Seguin. When the train bound in that direction blew its whistle, FROMME ran out of the house quickly and flagged down the train. As the train traffic grew, there was a schedule of at least eleven trains daily passing through Cibolo.

FROMME was a good businessman because he soon had a cotton gin, a lumber yard, and a hardware store which eventually was taken over by his son, Frank. He also built a merchandise store in Bracken, which included a two-story building with a hotel on top. His business there was next to a saloon and quite profitable for some time.

By this point in 1880, several Mexican American families lived and worked in the Valley. They are listed as:

CERTINA, Ruiz, Michael
CONTRERES, Joseph, Michael
BARRIENTES, Camillo
CASTILLO, Antonio
ENSERIA, Joseph

African American farmers decreased in number:

JOHNSON, John
GRIGGS, Sam
RAINEY, Joseph
SNEED, Harrison
PETERS, Moses
CURTIS, Isaac
ANTHONY, Beverly

THE POST OFFICE

The Post Office at Valley had been discontinued in June 1867 but re-established in December of the same year with George BERGFIELD as postmaster. He held the position until 1875 and is not listed in the 1880 census, so it is probable that he grew tired of it sometime after 1875 when Otto MEINERS took over. Otto had clerked in general merchandise stores since he was nineteen. Four years later in 1879, August SCHMITZ was given the title of postmaster.

The census in 1880 counted many people in the area as being in the Santa Clara area, but there were still people who called themselves residents of Lower Valley. SCHLATHER continued with the store until 1882 when he sold it to Charles FROMME who had been living in Santa Clara.

FROMME, a successful businessman, had the finances to buy the store and run it. SCHLATHER decided he could make money with another enterprise—a saloon—and built one that also had a dance hall with living quarters upstairs.

In 1886, FROMME built a rock building beside the railroad tracks and later added a second building with a cellar for storage. He took the job of postmaster in 1883 after August PFEIL. FROMME then built a large home behind the store. He used the front room of this house for post office business until he later added a small room strictly for the post office. His house was the location for the first piano in Cibolo. He also had running water piped into the house from a small well by a windmill, which pumped it into an elevated cistern.

SCHOOLS

Schools were very important and opened as soon as any settlers were in the area. One of the first permanent schools recognized by the state in the Lower Valley began in 1877. However, school board minutes and reports had been kept from 1851 on. Since all schools in Guadalupe County had a number, this one was #37. Counties were to have schools for students between the ages of six and sixteen.

Each district in the county (Guadalupe had eleven at first) was to elect three trustees who were responsible to hire a teacher with good qualifications and high moral character, visit the school, discharge a teacher for improper conduct, and expel a student for misconduct. People of the district had to build a school and furnish it before they received any money.

The first teacher for the Valley seems to have been August SCHMITZ who was paid $30 monthly but received raises. Married to Margaretha STAPPER SCHMITZ in August 1860, he was paid $38.30 and $38.50 for two schools from the previous term in 1859 in the district but not Cibolo Valley. Appointees for school board of his school at that time were Jacob PFEIL and Swiss-born Melchior AMACHER who had property in San Antonio as well as the Valley and knew the value of careful bookkeeping. During the Civil War, schools received little funding since few could pay taxes. The records for Receipts and Disbursements for Public Free Schools in 1877-1878 show SCHMITZ taught four months at Long Valley, which was typical for a school

term. He worked as a postmaster and telegraph operator and to supplement his income to support his family of one son and five daughters. Three young sons died before 1870. The death of SCHMITZ in 1894 was a loss to the school and the community.

In Cibolo, a school was built west of town on private property where Oscar SAMUEL taught students before he became a minister of the church. He encouraged residents to have a school on church property, and he and English-born Henry EAST were teachers at the school. That building burned and was replaced by another. Teachers not associated with St. Paul's Church were Mr. AHR and Mr. William STAPPER. A one-room schoolhouse was erected in 1902, and twelve years later a second building was constructed to meet the demands of a growing enrollment. By 1913, eight men met to plan the building of a high school: R.A. PFEIL, Anton PFEIL, Dr. H. BENNING, Mr. ZENNER, Ernst SCHLATHER, Henry UHR, John FISCHER, and R.W. VORDENBAUM. Although plans were made and the county superintendent contacted, a bond election was not held until 1916. The vote was sixty-three for and nine against bonds for a new high school. Trustees F.W. WERNER, George SCHLATHER, and Alfred SAHM were awarded a contract for the building of a two-story brick structure. First graduates of the class of 1920 were Herbert SCHUELER, Olivia BOLTON, and George H. SCHLATHER. In 1921 – 1922 a teacher's salary had reached the sum of $100.00 for eight months.

Schools in Guadalupe County needed plans to exterminate rats. Prizes for individuals who brought in the most rat tails were $2.00, $1.00, and $.50 for first, second, and third places in each school. First prize for the school in the county which collected the most rat tails (the principal of each school tabulated the tails and then burned them) was $25.00 By the time the contest had ended, 103,700 rat tails had been collected.

There was also the novelty of unique rats. Edwin HILD brought into the office of the Seguin Enterprise, a six-legged rat which was killed on the

Max BLUME farm by Otto PETERS, Will PETERS, G. BLUME, and himself.

ECONOMIC CONDITIONS

Farmers continued to raise several crops with wheat crop production on the rise from 1876 through 1880. However, a rust or blight attacked the crop in 1880, and farmers decided that wheat was too uncertain a crop to continue to plant. They began to concentrate on cotton.

Economic conditions seemed to be doing well at this point in Cibolo. A typical plot of 272 acres sold for $2400.50 with $900 as down payment. The first house in Cibolo built without being on farmland or connected by walls to a business enterprise was built in 1886 by William KEULER who had only come to the United States and Texas in 1879.

On August 20th 1886, a terrible storm and hurricane came roaring through the county. Edward DIETZ, the first son after six daughters, and four more children born after him of Ferdinand and Elizabeth STAPPER DIETZ, later spoke about the considerable rain which began early in the morning and blew down signs and fences. Large trees were uprooted, roofs came off houses, and some houses were even moved off their foundations. Most of the windmills in the area were blown down. There was no loss of life although the editor of the paper reported that a pauper on the south side of the Cibolo was said to have "died of fright."

Ferdinand and his brother came first to the county to work as cowboys for Jacob de CORDOVA at the stage stop which was at his house. Nine German bachelors bought property and built a kind of dormitory/house for themselves before they eventually married and started families.

County government business continued as Grand Jury Members in 1888 were Joseph STAPPER, John HAECKER, and Louis VORDENBAUM. They were to receive $10 for their days of service on the jury. HAECKER was the father of thirteen children, but he was bested by VORDENBAUM who had fifteen.

Photo taken in 1984 after restoration of the Haecker home built by Henry Haecker in 1880. Photo courtesy of Bonnie George.

August BLUMBERG, whose family came to Texas in 1845, built a store building on the north side of the tracks. He and his family were instrumental in developing land around McQueeney and Marion and became an important cog in the business world of the Valley. Frederick "Fritz" WERNER built the first blacksmith shop around 1893 with help from his brother Albert WERNER. It would become a general store at a later date. He next built a large two-story tin building on the corner of Main Street and FM78 used to store hardware, harnesses, and buggy parts brought by the trail, assembled, and moved up by elevator to the top of the building. Hacks and buggies became popular just at the turn of the century. Hacks were square with curtains on the sides rolled up in good weather and let down when it rained. Farm wagons were still in use but not as much.

Citizens took their turn at the grand jury in Seguin in 1891: Otto BROTZE, Henry RABE, and Philip SHRAUB. Marksmen from Cibolo Valley who won prizes at the 1891 San Geronimo Schutzen Verein or Shooting Society against eighty contestants included: J. HILBERT who won an umbrella, Friedolin WERNER, father of Fritz and Albert, who won a bowl and pitcher, and Henry ADAMS who won a wicker chair. Sunday afternoons from March to October was the time for gun clubs such as the one at San Geronimo. The target range was two hundred yards. Each club gave a monthly medal, but to be kept permanently, the medal had to be won three times in succession.

At this point, William KEULER began his work as a photographer and took pictures in a tent built in his yard. Later he constructed a building with a roof made of glass. However, since very cold water was needed to develop his pictures, he found it difficult to continue the work. He became the Justice of the Peace for the area, probably the first, as well as Cibolo's passenger freight agent.

Travel was still difficult even with a railroad. At first the trip from the VALLEY to SCHERTZ took over an hour by wagon. It was a curving, curling road on the north side of the railroad that went through several private farms with gates that had to be opened and closed. Several years after the railroad came through, the county decided to build FM 78. All male taxpayers were required to work at least one day of the year on the construction of the road or be subject to a fine.

Richard PFEIL built a wood frame store that did well as a general merchandise store. Son of August and Anna Maria STAPPER PFEIL, Richard would stay in the merchandise business the rest of his life even after relocating from Cibolo. Somewhere around 1894, Miss Alwinne FROMME, daughter of Charles FROME and Miss Theresa BROTZE, daughter of Otto BROTZE, occupied a small building that had been built on the west side of Main Street. It was a millinery store that gave the ladies of Cibolo their Sunday hats. They were probably not as elaborate as some worn in San Antonio, but they were pleasant straw hats with a colorful ribbon or a bonnet style with nice lace.

Some writers used the name of CIBOLO in their works. O. HENRY (William Sidney Porter) wrote a short story "The Higher Abdication" in which the setting begins in San Antonio and then moves to the CIBOLO ranch. The story tells about a prosperous business venture with six cowboys plus the owner and his son. He describes the "irregular, sloping stretch of prairie mixed with mesquite and chaparral," so it appears to be farther west of the VALLEY.

In "Round the Circle," O. Henry again has a Texas setting and describes the "narrow stretch of smiling valley, upholstered with a rich mat of green, curly mesquite grass," but again this description takes place between the Nueces and Frio Rivers. He does write of the Germans in Fredericksburg and any number of events which take place in San Antonio.

When Teddy Roosevelt assembled his Rough Riders in San Antonio on June 14, 1898, Cibolo residents kept track of what was happening. It was mostly cowboys who became a part of the group, but the young men in Guadalupe County were still interested in what was going to take place in faraway San Juan.

The election of 1896 was a milestone as the

Cibolo area voted for William McKinley. It was the first-time voters had picked anyone other than a Democrat since the end of Reconstruction.

As the new century dawned, changes became evident in Cibolo. Fritz WERNER decided to go into the gasoline business and built one of the first "filling stations" in the county, operating the Gulf Station until 1970, the oldest continually operating Gulf station in the United States. The filling station still stands at the corner of Main and old FM 78. His next step was to open a Ford car agency for the popular Ford Model T.

In 1900, English-born John HICKS became postmaster as he handled business in his own general merchandise store.

At this point, farming continued to be the most important part of Cibolo life. More than 455 farms existed from Marion to LaVernia to Selma to Cibolo Creek. Other occupations in the area consisted of cobbler, freight driver, well digger, telegraph operator (two), cook, railroad agent, night watchman, railroad porter, barber, hostler, ginner (seven), merchants-salesmen (twenty), saloon keeper (three), bartender (two), bookkeeper (two), carpenter (five), minister (two), teacher (seven), blacksmith (five), lumber dealer, saddlemaker, beer wagon driver, butcher (three), apothecary, and tank scraper.

Beekeepers were present in all of Guadalupe County because honey was an important staple of country life. In a nearby community, Ludwig STACHELHAUSEN was known for his ability with bees while in Cibolo John GEHELS had many bee hives and was called the "Beeman" by most people.

When the first Confederate Pension plan was offered, applications were received and approved for several Cibolo families. They included Maria VORDNEBAUM, widow of William, Heinrich GROBE, Jacob SCHRAUB, and Henrietta WEIDNER, widow of Henry.

By the 1900 census the number of African American families were about the same, seventeen. The number of Mexican-American families was much larger numbering sixty or more. Many were working on the farms of those in Cibolo, but others were involved with blacksmithing, cabinet making, or groundskeeping.

THE TOWN OF CIBOLO

Farmers continued to plant cotton and corn, so there was a need for a gin. An early gin was built by George SCHLATHER on the north side of the railroad tracks.

Sometime later, Julian STAPPER and Hugo SCHAEFER built a gin near Crescent Bend. Schaefer was the son of Texas Ranger Robert SCHAEFER and Agnes PFEIL SCHAEFER. By 1901 SCHAEFER went into partnership with Karl FROMME on another gin.

Water for the steam-powered gins could be hauled by wagons from Cibolo Creek. It was a constant line of wagons going to the creek and then to the gin causing a cloud of dust in the air during the peak harvest times of early fall. Cotton was certainly important as more than 100,000 acres were planted in the county.

Henry UHR built the first two-story building in Cibolo near the railroad tracks. It housed a butcher shop and the second floor was used for lodge meetings. Butchers were necessary in the community, and Alwin HAECKER and Hugo WEST worked in that department. Later the building became an ice house. In 1909, twenty-five-year-old Robert VORDENBAUM became postmaster working out of his father's business.

In 1913 two notable events took place. The Cibolo Creek was out of its banks and caused heavy flooding in the area. On September 15, 1913 a bank was established with a total capital of $12,000. The front room of the Karl FROMME home served as its operation center until a building could be erected. Arthur SCHRAUB donated the land next to his store, and a seventeen-foot strip of land was bought from the church. In 1914, the original Cibolo Bank was built with furniture made by Edward MEYER. With no heating in the colder winter days, cashier A. G. JANSEN had to wear an overcoat and gloves. First officers of the bank were C.E. TIPPS, President; Robert VORDENBAUM, Vice-President; Anton PFEIL, Secretary; and A.G. SCHRAUB. Charles KIEFER was the first cashier but was succeeded by Victor JANSEN after two weeks. His assistants later were Henry and O.P. SCHNABEL, William HAYS, and Mr. JANSEN.

MEYER was a man of many abilities. Besides

carpentry, he owned a garage on the north side of the railroad tracks and was an expert in replacing tops on touring cars and roadsters. He sold gas, oil, tires, everything a car owner might need. His wife Johanna MEYER operated a fine boarding house in their home where she served excellent meals to her boarders and to salesmen passing through Cibolo.

A saloon stood next to the bank for those who needed to play a game of dominoes or have a drink. John Thomas MURPHY, first proprietor, named the saloon the PEARL Bar after his wife Pearl Thornton MURPHY. The player piano was the source of much entertainment. Later owners were Oscar SCHRAUB, Tommy MEEK, and Rudy VOIGHT who changed the name to VOIGHT's PLACE or RUDY'S. Another saloon owned by Henry UHR changed hands and brought financial problems between UHR and A.G. SCHRAUB resulting in a law suit taken before the courts.

Some of the dairies produced quality milk, and one owned by Otto BROTZE received a passing mark in the Milk Analysis from the Report of Dairy and Food Commissioner in 1916. That same year, Ernest SCHLATHER took the job of postmaster and held it for the next thirty-four years. Mail continued to be distributed in businesses all over Cibolo such as John HICKS' general store until a permanent building was constructed in 1961.

Electric lights and electricity were a real curiosity for folks in Cibolo. Sidney VORDENBAUM had them installed in his drug store on June 27, 1917 while Edward MEYER was the first to have them in a home. R.J MOTSCH had the first electric fan. He began as a machinist in one of the gins until he eventually owned part of one himself.

By 1920 FROMME's Gin had begun to operate as the Farmer's Gin with near eighty stockholders, all farmers from the Cibolo area. Prior to that time, John George SCHLATHER SR. had also built a gin near the present location of Cibolo's water tower. Gins were now becoming "modern" with improvements such as blowers.  Up to that point, ginners had to carry the cotton up to the gin with baskets, a slow process in which farmers who brought in the cotton often lent a hand. Also, electricity replaced the steam operation. An article in the 1930 *Guadalupe Gazette* stated, "The ginner throws the switch and the thing goes—he throws it off and it stops. It isn't necessary for the mechanic to know what makes the darn thing run without steam. It DOES run!"

E.A. BAKER had a shoe repair shop on Main Street. He also repaired leather collars, harnesses and lines for farmers who were still using horse-drawn farm machinery. Emil RAWE began his blacksmith business in 1926 just east of there. Even

though he also worked on cars, blacksmithing and wheel-wright work provided his main income. He had learned his trade by working with Albert WERNER and gained valuable knowledge at a young age

Another filling station and garage was built by Emil WIEDERSTEIN in 1928 and managed by his sons. There were two tourist cottages near this spot for those visiting in the area. In 1924, Emil WIEDERSTEIN and Ewald PFEIL opened the Cibolo Lumber Company. Cabinetmakers, Charles KIERUM and Alwin WIEDERSTEIN became frequent customers.

Cibolo Lumber Company Photo
courtesy of Cassandra Kearns

By this point, the original store that August BLUMBERG built on the north side of the tracks had been sold to Emil HARBORTH. The store was so big that HARBORTH made the back of it into an apartment for his family's living quarters. He sold dry goods, groceries, boots, shoes, hats and practically anything that farmers might need. The store was later moved to a different location. Otto GROBE owned another merchandise store. He had previously been in the brick business. He and his brother August GROBE bought stock and began their business.

Old Cibolo Lumber Photo courtesy of Jim Burdett

Eventually the family moved the stock, and the store was known as C&E Grocery.

The 1930's brought Depression years, which meant difficult times for everyone in the United States. Nationwide, a number close to 24 percent were out of work. In 1933, many Cibolo farmers had to plow up the cotton they had planted, each having at least sixteen acres in the contract made to the government. The Committee in charge of carrying out the government plan was made up of Ewald PFEIL, Hilmer STAPPER, A, R. SCHRAUB, Robert DIETZ, and O.G. WIEDERSTEIN. Over 30,274 acres in Guadalupe County were in the program. But small businesses did their best to survive and improve services to Cibolo. The first beauty shop was owned by Adaline DOERR who became the bride of William EASON. Mrs. Bebieda CLARMER SCHUL operated a laundry specializing in good hot water for clothing.

The Red Ball Cafe on the corner of Main and

Loop 539, across from St. Paul's Church, was owned by Mr. and Mrs. Trotti. It was known for its fine home-cooked lunches prepared by Vera KEULER TROTTI and Velaska KEULER. Their chili was famous, and many a salesman and tourist stopped to get a bowl of that chili. This café was a place for gathering of locals. There was always a hot pot of coffee along with local gossip keeping the stools warm. The Red Ball Bus Line made it's stop there along with stops in other small towns. When it came time to tear the building down to make way for progress, Ed Ling purchased it and moved it to his property on FM 78 beside Neimetz Park.

Ernst SCHLATHER, who had been a cotton buyer, opened his own grocery business on the corner of Main and PFEIL Streets. It was known as the Red and White Grocery. Shortly thereafter, he began a corn shelling operation, a grain elevator and storage company that became known as E.H. SCHLATHER and Sons.

The Depression left its mark on all the families in Cibolo. At first, the Stock Market crash didn't seem to slow down the economy of surrounding cities of San Antonio and New Braunfels, but days turned into weeks, months, and years when prices went down on every product and money became scarce. By 1932, homeless families camped along the banks of any river or creek like the Cibolo. Men who rode the railroads to anywhere they thought there might be work would often stop at the Cibolo station and go to nearby farms to see if any job was available in exchange for food. They marked the fences of most farms with signs known to all the rail riders: danger, good water, kind woman, good place for food, barking dogs, unsafe area, barn for sleeping. They would usually go to the back door of a farmhouse, knock, and ask for a job or simply ask for food. Housewives would give them bread or biscuits with syrup. A common food item was "Hoover gravy" which was made with water not milk.

At this time, the continuous planting of cotton had depleted the soil, and the number of bales being produced had dropped. For this reason, farmers began to concentrate more on livestock but also planted corn.

Rural telephone companies branched out, and Cibolo had one that involved certain rules and code for a customer's service. The phone was to be used from 5:00 a.m. to 10:00 p.m. It could not be used during storms. Certain rings were for each individual customer, and someone listening had to pay attention for his or her ring. For example:

SCHUEL, Adolph—#24—long, short
SCHERTZ, Eugene—#7—2 long

SCHLATHER, Leo—#45—short, long, short
SCHLATHER Store—#50—long, short, long

The rural telephone system would hit its peak in 1927 and be replaced with some of the programs that came in the New Deal from Washington.

Cibolo Mercantile Company or the "farmer's store" as it was often called was formed with eighty-six stockholders and Harry SCHARTZ as manager. The business did well for some time but ran into some fierce competition as the area began to grow.

Cibolo Grain Company was organized in 1924 by Ewald OSWALD, Alfred PFEIL, Julian STAPPER, and Herbert WEYEL. The company bought and sold corn. Earlier, Ernst SCHLATHER had erected a temporary loading-unloading chute to take care of farmers who brought in loads of corn during the harvest season.

Sometime after the 1930 census, Harrison SNEED, the oldest living black resident of Cibolo at more than eighty-five years of age, died. He came to the county after the Civil War and raised his family here.

World War II—it was a difficult time for all of America and certainly Cibolo. Young men were called to serve their country, and those at home helped in every way possible. In April of 1942 rationing of sugar began, and soon after that meat, butter, cheese, and canned milk would join the list.

Everyone was encouraged to save everything they could around the home and use it to recycle for the war effort. War Bonds were sold.

The weather added to an uneasy situation. On August 31, 1942, a strong tropical storm hit Guadalupe County on a Sunday morning. This was a result of a hurricane that had struck the coast the day before. Guadalupe county and San Antonio had endured 50 to 70 mph wind gusts for as much as five hours when the storm moved to Cibolo. Old timers often called storms such as this "general rains," but this one peeled back tin roofs, uprooted old trees, destroyed telephone service and electricity, and caused extensive property damage. At nearby Randolph Field, airmen held down planes for hours pressing on the wings to keep them from blowing away. Most of the next few days were spent in cleaning up the debris left from the storm, but further destruction came on September 4 when more than five inches of rain fell. Those who had not had time to repair windows or roofs were hit once more. In Refugio County, the storm brought nine inches of rain.

Cibolo firetruck 1957

The declaration of victory after World War II saw a new spirit hit the county as Cibolo residents went back to the job of raising crops and rebuilding their lives. A number of new residents moved into the area.

With the help of the Grange, the Cibolo Volunteer Fire Department was organized in March 1956. The first board of directors included Marvin KIERUM, Alwin LIECK, James MEEK, E.C. WIEDERSTEIN, Carl FROMME, Edgar VORDENBAUM, Tommy MEEK, George SCHLATHER, Jesse DOANE, Emil RAWE, and Charles FLING. A financial drive resulted in a fire truck and a fire station by September 1957. First Fire Chief was Alvin LIECK. A ladies' auxiliary was organized in 1958 which contributed to equipment for the men and the fire station. Cibolo's pumper teams captured first place in several competitions.

On October 20, 1965 Cibolo voted to become an independent township with the first mayor being M.O. GROOMS. Councilmen were Ted DYKES Fred NIEMETZ, Carl BISER, D.O. and Carl TROTTI, and Alwin LIECK. The first city secretary was Linda LING.

Linda Ling Bates – First City Clerk working on the typewriter from 1968.

City hall was first located in the First City Bank that now sits beside the jewelry store on Main.

Cibolo saw many community projects accomplished over the years. The Cibolo City Park came into being when the city acquired thirteen acres on Cibolo Creek which had once belonged to Leon SCHLATHER. The community cleared the land, renovated an old farm house, constructed ball diamonds, and other facilities.

An Interscholastic League ruling in 1972 stated Texas high schools could not have a live mascot. Samson was the Clemens High School mascot, so the Cibolo State Bank located on FM 78 volunteered to keep him and built a corral on property.

It was these types of community actions that made Cibolo a pleasant place to live and work, and residents never dreamed it would turn from one hundred residents in 1890 into one of the fastest growing areas in the Hill Country with a population in the 2010 U.S. census of 15,349. "The City of Choice" has become the slogan for Cibolo, and its rich history reflects the choices made by pioneers and working people as they went about their daily lives. In the future, it will be amazing to watch the accomplishments and growth of the place where bison once grazed.

WORLD WAR I IN CIBOLO AND SCHERTZ

Just as World War I broke out, some anti-German feelings grew in the area due to the infamous Zimmerman letter, a letter from the German ambassador to Mexican authorities which said if Mexico would join with Germany against the Allies, then Germany would help Mexico in recovering territorial areas lost through the years. This would, of course, be taking in some of southern Texas.

Those of German descent sometimes called the other settlers a "Raggedy" which meant they were non-German. The Anglo settlers sometimes called the Germans "Square Heads" or "Dutchmen." But German heritage families tried to show their loyalty to the United States every way they could. In schools, for at least ten minutes a day, teachers taught patriotism. Menus were designed to show sacrifice when there was wheatless Monday, meatless Tuesday, porkless Thursday. Citizens bought Liberty Bonds, Victory Bonds, and War Savings stamps. A typical cake recipe had no eggs or milk and was very light on shortening; other ingredients used were simple foods around the home such as brown sugar or raisins.

Men who enlisted went to either Camp Travis or Camp Bowie, but the numbers were slow at first. On March 1, 1918, the *Guadalupe Gazette* called for more volunteers and reported that it was a mark of true patriotism. Allotments by the government assigned $15 for an enlisted married man. For one child in the family, the check would be $25 and for two, it was $32.50. Nurses were in short supply for the army.

A man from another county who had made critical remarks of those who were collecting for the Red Cross effort was tarred and feathered and given twelve hours to get out of town.

On December 17, 1918, the *Guadalupe Gazette* advised that those who did volunteer should take only a suitcase with them and a small amount of clothing. The government would give them what they needed. There was a rationing nation-wide of meat, bread, flour, sugar, and butter.

After the Draft Registration Selective Service Act passed, three registration periods were set up. The third was in September 1918 for all eligible men between the ages of eighteen and forty-five. Those designated for this list on their draft enrollment as being from Schertz are marked "Schertz." Those with no marking are shown on this list as being from Cibolo.

Names on the Draft Registration Selective Service Act List from Cibolo and Schertz:

"A"

Achterberg, Edgar—21, farmer
Albarado, Gregorio—27, works for Stapper
Albardo, Pedro—21, works for Bielstein
Albrecht, Hermann—21, works for Wiedner
Albrecht, John—44, works for Brotze
Aleman, Phillips—29, works for Koepp
Aleman, Thomas—25, works for Schlather
Aleman, Fernando—20, works for Amacher
Alvarado, Caterino—30, works for Krickhelm
Amacher, Edwin—26, farmer, constable
Amacher, Joe Otto—24, self-employed
Arizpe, Salvador—23, Blacksmith
Aranke, Ernst—23, farmer

"B"

Barsch, Wilhemund—39, dentist
Bauer, August—44, farmer
Beck, Alfred—18, farmer, Schertz
Beck, Henry—42, clerk at Schertz Mercantile, Schertz
Behrens, Alfred—26, farmer
Behrens, Herman—29, farmer
Behrens, Otto—32, farmer
Bielstein, Paul—21, works for Bielstein
Boettcher, Herman—35, on poor farm, works for Vordenbaum
Boettcher, Phillip—40, on poor farm, works for Vordenbaum
Bolton, Fritz—29, works for Schwab
Bolton, Edward—22, laborer
Bolton, Ferdinand—28, barber, tailor
Bolton, Frank—26, barber

Bolton, Frido Otto—25, farmer
Bolton, George—35, enlisted in 2nd Texas Cavalry
Bonilla, Jose—40, works for Wiederstein
Borgfeld, Herman—34, owns repair shop, Schertz
Bowermann, Robert—40, farmer
Brotze, Curt—42, carpenter
Buede, Edmund—42, farmer

"C"
Carle, Alexander—27, works at RR station
Carnisallis, Thomas—20, works for Werner
Chisum, Roy—34, RR agent
Clarence, Hugo—28, blacksmith
Cothan, Christian—32, physician, Schertz

"D"
Dietz, August—21, self-employed
Dietz, Robert—40, farmer
Doerr, Louis—23, chauffeur

"E"
Ebert, August—45, farmer
Ebert, Edmond—32, clerk at Schertz Mercantile, Schertz
Ebert, Hugo—30, works at Schertz Garage, Schertz
Ebert, Willie—21, clerk at Schertz Mercantile, Schertz

"F"
Farella, Francisco—35, works for Schlather
Fenske, Adolph—39, works for Korasky, Schertz
Fenske, Edmond—27, cook, Schertz
Fenske, Willie—18, laborer, Schertz
Fischer, Daniel—34, manager of lumber yard, Schertz
Fischer, Frank—30 works for Borgfeld

Fisher, Georg—45, farmer
Fromme, Frank—42, merchant

"G"
Garcia, Antonio—24, works for Reinmayer
Gehrels, John August—38, engineer
Gerlich, Smil—42, merchant/postmaster, Schertz
Gonzales, Feliz—21, works for Shertz
Grobe, Albert—30, farmer, Schertz
Grobe, August—33, merchant at A.H. Grobe Co., Schertz
Grobe, Oscar—28, laborer, Schertz
Guzman, Santiago—35, works for Wiederstein

"H"
Haecker, Alvin J.—23, works for Vordenbaum
Haecker, Antonius J.—18, farmer
Haecker, Frederick—42, farmer
Haecker, Gustav H.—57, farmer
Haecker, Harry—22, farmer
Haecker, Henry—21, farmer
Haecker, Herman—32, farmer
Haecker, John—41, farmer
Haecker, Oscar—19, enlisted in NST, Captain Newton's
Haecker, Rudolph—38, works for Pfanstiel
Haecker, Walter A.—34, farmer
Harmes, Louis—38, farmer
Hernando, Anastacio—38, works for Vordenbaum
Hernandez, Nasario—30, works for Vondenbaum
Hernandez, Manuel—23, works for Dulbrig, Schertz
Hernandez, Sabiacio—34, section hand on RR
Herrera, Pillareo—26, works for Friesenhahn
Hibaben, Refugio—41, farmer
Hierholzer, Benton—18, works for Hierholzer

Hierholzer, Walter—21, farmer
Hild, Edwin—24, farmer
Hildebrand, Arthur—29, works for Fey
Hilbert, Willy—39, blacksmith, Schertz

"I"

"J"
Jacon, Eliseo—24, works for Haecker
James, William—46, laborer, Schertz
Jansen, Adolph G.—40, cashier at Cibolo Bank
Jonas, Richard—29, telephone operator for Farmers Rural Telephone, Schertz
Jonas, Robert—23, farmer

"K"
Kallies, Otto—38, ginner, Schertz
Katt, Erich A.—37, farmer
Kierun, Charles—28, works at Schertz Garage, Schertz
Kircher, Edwin—23, works for Birkner
Klegfield, Otto—25, pharmacist at Cockran Drug, Schertz
Klug, Paul—39, farmer
Kneupper, Henry—37, carpenter
Koch, Christian—41, merchant, Schertz Mercantile, Schertz
Koel, Frank—29, telegraph operator/station manager, Schertz
Koehler, Walter—21, farmer
Korensk, Fred—25, rural mail carrier
Kraft, Harry—24, works for Fey
Kramer, Walter Emil—32, farmer, Schertz
Kreusler, Christian—24, farmer
Kreusler, William—25, farmer
Krickhahm, Rudolph—41, farmer
Kriewald, Paul—41, works for Vordenbaum

Kropp, Albert H.—34, farmer
Kropp, Edgar—25, farmer
Krueger, William—30, farmer

"L"
Lambrecht, Dan J.—30, farmer
Lambrecht, Louis C.—27, farmer
Leal, Santiago—24, works for Neubauer
Lopes, Gregorio—24, works for Pfeil

"M"
Martinez, Braulio—27, works for Schuemann
Martinez, Fidell-24, works for Grobe
Martinez, Jesus—27, works for Wesch
Martinez, Thomas—works for Stapper
Martinez, Jose Paderes—43, bricklayer, Schertz
Martinez, Juan Vereal—19, works for Dietz
Mayer, Peter Anton—34, garage man
McMenamie, Perry—25, visiting family, Schertz
Melchor, Bartolo—19, works for Fisenbalm
Mendiolo, Jose—34, works for Schwab
Mergle, Gustau Carl—21, farmer
Mergele, John George—19, farmer
Mergele, Walter T.—43, works for Maske
Miller, Max—37, works for Neubauer
Minola, Deofila—27, works for Pfeil
Moehring, Christ—24, works for Jonas, Schertz
Molana, Rainon—39, works for Schertz
Moltz, John Henry—39, teaches at Cibolo High
Moltz, Theodore—26, teaches at Lower Valley School
Motsch, Rudolph—40, cotton ginner
Mueller, Henry Robert—20, farmer
Mueller, Wilhelm—22, farmer

Muniz, Encarcion—24, laborer
Munoz, Marco—35, works for Weyel
Myers, Edward C.—38, garage man

"N"
Nunnes, Modesto—29, works for Pfeil

"O"
Orth, Charles Jr.—18, works for Orth
Ortiz, Sal—27, works for Botten, Schertz
Otto, Wilfred—29, bartender for Gerlich, Schertz

"P"
Peres, Eurebio—22, works for Vordenbaum
Pfannstiel, Theodore—39, farmer
Pfeil, Anton T.—38, farmer
Pfeil, Ewald—30, farmer
Pfeil, Henry—23, farmer
Pfeil, Herbert—43, farmer
Pfeil, Oswald—38, farmer
Pfeil, Richard—42, merchant
Procknow, Emil A.—45, farmer

"R"
Rabe, William—40, teacher, Green Valley School
Rawe, Emil—28, blacksmith
Real, Fritz—27, clerk, assistant postmaster, Schertz
Real, Willis—26, baker, Schertz
Reiley, Adolph—33, farmer
Reiley, August—30, farmer
Reininger, Edward—39, farmer
Reininger, Harry—38, farmer
Reininger, Louis—34, farmer

Reininger, Tony—18, works for Reininger
Reyes, Franlio—37, works for Jonas
Reyes, Moises—32, works for Kramer
Ricos, Manuel—23, works for Vordenbaum
Rittmann, Gustav—36, laborer
Rodriguez, Leonaldo—25, works for Haecker
Rocha, Roman—38, works for Bucke

"S"
Sanchez, Mateo—38, works for Dietz, Schertz
Santos, Nicalos—27, works for Jonas
Saldanyo, Leondra—38, works for Jonas
Sassmanhausen, Louis—34, farmer
Schertz, Arthur—22, farmer, Schertz
Schertz, Ferdinand—45, farmer, Schertz
Schertz, Walter—28, farmer, Schertz
Schlather, Elmer—20, enlisted in NCF (Captain Newton)
Schlather, Erich—18, student at A & M
Schlather, Leonhard—28, farmer
Schnabel, Henry—18, assistant bank cashier at Cibolo Bank
Schneider, Albert—21, farmer
Schneider, Ferdinand—41, farmer
Schneider, Willie—19, farmerSchraub, Arthur—26, merchant
Schraub, Edwin—29, farmer
Schraub, Henry—26, farmer
Schraub, Richard—32, works for Vordenbaum
Schraub, Walter—22, farmer
Schueler, Herbert—18, enlisted, 2nd Texas Cavalry, Captain Hill
Schenemann, William—37, farmer
Schwab, Alex—44, farmer
Schwab, Ulis—20, farmer
Schwab, Alvin—21, farmer
Schwab, Eduard—37, farmer

Cibolo Texas • The Early Years

Seiler, Eddie—30, farmer
Seiler, Emile—43, farmer
Seiler, Hugo—22, auto mechanic, Schertz
Seiler, Jacob—20, farmer
Seiler, Otto—22, farmer
Sifuentes, Inez—33, works for Sassmanhausen
Solis, Marcos—45, works for Jiga
Solis, Sesario—24, works for Bauer
Solis, Fiburcio—23, works for Wesch
Stapper, Hilmer—23, farmer
Stapper, John Robert—36, farmer
Stapper, Otto—32, farmer
Stolte, Bodo—18, farmer
Stolte, Edward—26, farmer
Stolte, Hugo—26, merchant
Stolte, Walter—33, farmer
Suarres, Juan—34, works for Pfannstiel
Sucero, Espetacio—25, works at creamery

"T"
Tolle, Fritz—41, farmer
Trevino, Gregorio—27, works for Jacobi

"U"
Urias, Hennaro—34, works for Stolte
Urias, Pedro—36, works for Stolte

"V"
Villareal, Joe—33, works for Fisher
Villareal, Valentino—26, works for Birkman, Schertz
Vogel, Carl—36, farmer
Vordenbaum, Frederick—44, farmer
Vordenbaum, Gustavo—38, farmer

Vordenbaum, Julius—37, farmer
Vordenbaum, S.G.—21, farmer, Schertz
Vordenbaum, Willie—41, merchant

"W"
Weir, Jamie—24, farmer
Weir, Johnnie—19, farmer
Weir, Reuben—21, farmer
Weller, Alvin—20, farmer
Werner, Albert J.—41, blacksmith
Werner, Fridolin—33, farmer
Wesch, Alfred—24
Wesch, Willie—32, farmer
Wheeler, James—21, works for Barkner, Schertz
Wiederstein, Albert—41, farmer
Wiederstein, Bruno—19, farmer, Schertz
Wiederstein, Emil—37, farmer
Wiedner, Adolph—20, farmer
Wiedner, Emil—37, farmer
Wiedner, Adolph—20, farmer
Wiedner, Charles—34, farmer
Wiedner, Herman—26, farmer
Wiedner, Louis—26, farmer
Wilburn, Bird—29, works for Jonas
Wooten, Edward—44, farmer
Wurst, Hugo—35, butcher

"X-Y"

"Z"
Zimmerman, Charley—22, farmer
Zuercher, Charles—32, works for Kneupper
Zunker, Ernst—34, works for Wiederstein

The Roster of the White National Army was published in 1918. Names below were on the list as well as the Selective Act List.

Dates for lists were from September 4, 1917 to September 4, 1918.

> Achterberg, Edgar
> Alwin, George Schwab
> Ebert, William E.
> Haecker, Harry
> Mendiola, Deofilo
> Schlather, Elmer
> Schlather, Erich George
> Schlather, Leonard
> Schneider, Albert
> Listed for Co. "M," 141st Infantry
> Schraub, Walter
> Listed for Guadalupe Volunteers
> Bolton, Frido
> Fenske, Edmond
> Seiler, Edwin
> Listed as killed in action at St. Mihiel, France with Co. L, 36th Infantry
> Kraft, Helmut

As trouble grew into the conflict that marked World War I, most German-American communities such as Cibolo and Schertz were often in favor of remaining neutral. It was not altogether a political thought but also the question of massive loans and arms sales to the Allies. This was not an uncommon idea in places all over the United States.

As hostilities began, President Woodrow WILSON, president from 1913 – 1921, used a huge advertising campaign for war bonds, pro-war advertisements, and pamphlets, which defended America's place in going to war. But with the sinking of the Lusitania in 1915, some acts of espionage in the U.W., and the decoding of the Zimmermann note in January 1917, those who held strong opinions against the German-American population were pushed to new levels. The President had earlier questioned the loyalty of those who might have cultural ties to their mother countries. How could they be loyal was the thought whispered or even openly declared. Although the war officially began in July 1914, the United States did not declare war until April 6, 1917.

Before the Declaration of War, serious discussions had gone on in Cibolo and Schertz. An article in the *Sophienburg*, the German language newspaper in New Braunfels, written by an outsider remarked, "We consider it safe to assume that 90% of the people of the county are opposed to war…real Americanism is faintly understood."

Changes in Guadalupe County were noticeable. If there was a band concert or piano recital, Bach and Beethoven were no longer played. Ads for groceries showed cans of "liberty cabbage" rather than sauerkraut. Even dogs got into the act when Dachshunds were called "liberty hounds." Other changes were as ridiculous. The "frankfurter" that had begun to be popular was renamed the "liberty dog" and finally slid into the common phrase of "hot dog." And those people who suffered from German measles were said to be ill with "liberty measles."

Since many of the citizens of Cibolo and Schertz spoke fluent German, they were careful not to speak on the "party line" telephones or at church services unless they spoke English. In the Fredericksburg courthouse, the minutes were in German and English, so it became difficult to ask for previous records. If a high school such as Cibolo's had been teaching German as a foreign language requirement, it was no longer offered. There was a decrease in German fraternal lodges and membership. Festivals that had heralded German dance or music were postponed.

German newspapers in Germany were quick to declare that all people of German heritage wherever they lived owed allegiance to the Fatherland. In Cibolo and Schertz, they suffered through the names attached to them: "Hun," "Square Head," "Fritz," or "Dutchman."

One of the biggest attacks on them came from the American Protective League created in March 1917. It was a national surveillance system with 1200 units across America. A secret society, the membership gave every operative the authority to be a national police officer. The first aim of the APL was to survey public schools and report any "seditious and disloyal conversations." Those who didn't buy Liberty Bonds were considered anti-American and certainly anyone who tried to evade the draft was a "slacker" and should be watched carefully. In San Antonio, there were thirty-four investigations of sedition based on reports from the APL.

President Woodrow WILSON knew of the activities of the APL and had initially given his approval. However, he began to have misgivings and later spoke of the "dangerous" aspect of having a secret society.

Since their intense scrutiny was on those of German descent, it was a constant worry for those in Cibolo who thought their actions might be considered dangerous even if they were not. At its height, the APL had as many as 250,000 members who had no real legal authority but acted as though they did. A member of the APL could enter a home or business on a tip that there was some action or some person who was acting in an un-American way. In some areas, the Red Cross barred individuals with German-sounding last names from joining in fear of sabotage.

In Cibolo and Schertz, German heritage families tried to show their loyalty to the United States by devoting at least ten minutes a day in each school to teach patriotism. Menus were designed to show sacrifice with wheatless Monday, meatless Tuesday, and porkless Thursday. Citizens bought Liberty Bonds, Victory Bonds, and War Savings stamps.

In Texas, laws were passed by the state which made certain things punishable by fine and/or imprisonment: criticism of the U.S. government, the American flag, officers, or military uniforms. A fine could be given to a library which pictured Germany in a favorable light. Naturalized, but foreign-born, citizens were not permitted to vote.

Congress passed the Espionage Act in 1917. The Post Office could ban newspapers and magazines written in German, so that made it very difficult for any published material coming to homes in Schertz or Cibolo that was not in English. A person convicted of interfering with recruitment could face up to twenty years in prison and a fine of $10,000.

In May 1917, the *New Braunfels Herald* reported a loyalty parade held in New Braunfels featured General Joe PERSHING "where the citizens declared loyalty to our country and the flag and sent it to President WILSON."

In February of that same year, PERSHING assumed command of the Southern Depot and Fort Sam Houston in San Antonio. PERSHING himself was from German ancestors who had changed the spelling of their last name to make it sound more American.

At the same time, the Austin newspapers reported that German agents were encouraging discontent and insurrection among the black and

Mexican population. Federal agents investigated the rumor that Mexican nationals planned to bomb the state capitol. In the Cibolo area, there were between twenty-five and thirty-five Mexican-Americans counted in the 1910 census as head of a household and included the surnames of ACUNA, MARTINEZ, LILA, LOSARIO, ELVARADO, NAVARRO, MORALES, HERNANDEZ, REYES, LOPEZ, GARCIA, RODRIGUEZ, GUERRA, and SUFUENTES. More than fifty Mexican-Americans are listed on the Draft Selective Service Act List from Cibolo and Schertz.

However, those who were worried about German-American sentiment toward the war would have been shocked to find out about a friend to Cibolo residents. William NEUNHOFFER, resident of Kerr County. A twenty-eight-year-old lawyer, NEUNHOFFER spoke fluent German, Spanish, and English and became a secret agent for the U.S. He went to Mexico City and posed as a "slacker" or draft dodger who had turned up in Mexico City at the Juarez Hotel which was a gathering place for German sympathizers and German agents. The conversations he had with others were loud enough for all to know he wanted to bomb the Panama Canal and do damage to any U.S. held territories. He was so convincing that some of the chief German spies brought him into their organization and made him aware of their plans. After the war, his testimony proved valuable in identifying many who wanted to do damage to the U.S.

Those who could not do the espionage work that NEUNHOFFER did were called to the Selective Service Office to register. If a man chose to enlist, he could expect to have an allotment for $15 monthly if he were married. A child in the family would increase the check to $25 and if two children, the amount would be $32.50. The *Guadalupe Gazette* reported those who did volunteer should take a suitcase with them that held a small amount of clothing because the government would give them what they needed.

Training camps were held at Camp Travis which had previously been known as Camp Wilson until August 1917. Draftees were encouraged to write letters to their home newspapers as an aid to morale. Ranking officers at the camp were regular army officers and junior officers were primarily Texas and Oklahoma graduates of officer-training camp. Later, so many were being brought in from other states that the numbers from Texas declined. Often there were illnesses and equipment shortages and sometimes a mounted patrol which dealt with those who might consider changing their minds and leave the camp. Influenza often turned into pneumonia.

Music was written to encourage loyalty among the citizens of the United States, and people in Cibolo assuredly heard the songs such as "Pack Up Your Trouble in Your Old Kit Bag,"

"Keep the Home Fires Burning," "It's a Long Way to Tipperary," "Over There," and "There's a Long, Long Trail A-Winding."

Another song which was even more close to home since the cover of the sheet music shows a soldier leaving the farm was "Good-by, Ma! Good-by, Pa! Good-by, Mule with yer old Heehaw."

> Goodby, Ma! Goodby, Pa!
> Goodby, Mule, with yer old heehaw!
> I may not know what th' war's about,
> but you bet, by gosh, I'll soon find out.
> An' O my sweetheart, don't you fear,
> I'll bring you a King fer a souvenir;
> I'll git you a Turk an' a Kaiser, too,
> An' that's about all one feller could do!

The verse describes the soldier as a "long, lean country gink from way out west" which fit many Cibolo and Schertz young men in the minds of those who lived elsewhere.

The Sedition Act of 1918 made it a federal offense to use "disloyal, profane, scurrilous or abusive language" about the Constitution, the government, American emblems, or the flag. It was a further extension of the Espionage Act.

An urgent call was made in local papers in May 1918 for more volunteers. The numbers who already volunteered was not as high as authorities wanted. Also, there was a shortage of nurses, so women who would consider training were offered a good monthly wage. But sales of Liberty Bonds were very high, more than $129,000 sold in one week in Guadalupe County. During the war there were four issues of Liberty Bonds: April 24, 1917; October 1, 1917; April 5, 1918; September 28, 1918. Each time period said the number of bonds sold to citizens to help pay for the war increased. Posters produced when the Liberty Bonds were sold called for patriotism, love of country, and an acute fear of the German soldiers with posters picturing German soldiers with huge, fierce faces committing acts of violence: "Halt the Hun," "Beat Back the Hun with Liberty Bonds," "Must Children Die and Mothers Plead in Vain," and "Remember Belgium."

Every soldier had a vocational assignment with complete history, experience, proficiency, all based on an interview with the local board. The distrust of German-American men from Cibolo and Schertz was evident in the assessments made of them in camp despite any background which would prove their loyalty. A letter from the local board in Comal County states the feelings shared by most Hill Country boards.

August 31, 1918

From Local Board for Comal County, Texas
To: Major Frank S. Roberts, Chief Int. Off.,
Camp Travis, Texas

Subject: Inventory of men from Comal County on basis of loyalty

In answer to yours of recent date the Local Board for Comal County, in consultation with the Government Appeal Agent and the Sheriff of the county, have carefully checked over the men in the army with regard to their absolute loyalty.

The difficulties encountered in this undertaking may be imagined when it is taken into consideration that the citizenship of this county, Comal, is almost entirely of German ancestry, and even considerably of German birth and that this citizenship has zealously kept alive the German language, has surrounded its children with German influence from the cradle—songs, folklore, church, and both civic and moral ideals. We must state that real Americanism is but faintly understood on the part of the majority of the people. We consider it safe to assume that ninety percent of the people of the county are opposed to our present war on the grounds that is "only the purpose of dragging the English chestnut out of the fire;" that it was brought about by Wall Street; that it was unjustifiable to thwart Germany from her just fruits of a successful war of defense;" etc. etc. Of course, this sort of talk is not open, but this is the prevailing undercurrent of sentiment.

With the younger men, this feeling is not so strong, but the effect upon them of the views of their elders cannot be successfully gauged. We have made every effort to classify these men accurately, bearing in mind the seriousness of the matter—of the injustice we might do them, and on the other hand of the possible serious import to the Nation. The classification was based on home environment, known verbal expressions of the men themselves since our entry into the war.

By: R.H. Marrs, Secretary

From the secretary's letter, it seems all boards were doubtful concerning the German-American men and were unlikely to place them in positions that called for them to be in charge of camp security. An example of this is the case of Percy VALENTINE WETZ who was drafted in June of 1918. His family's farm was between Bracken and Schertz, and he farmed some of his own land. According to his draft card he was of medium build, short, brown eyes, and light brown hair. Once at Camp Travis, he applied for positions with security details but was turned down despite his abilities to handle firearms and do the job. Fred JOHNSTON of the APL had requested of the War Department that all men with German-sounding surnames be investigated in a stricter way than the usual soldiers. At Camp Travis, PERCY was turned down because he was from the area that was considered untrustworthy and a copy of an earlier letter from Frank ROBERTS was included in his file. He was then sent to Camp Lee in Virginia to be trained in veterinary school where he would not be in a place that needed security. Sadly, he contracted pneumonia and died there. His obituary gave the details.

> Nov. 8, 1918
>
> Percy W. WETZ, son of Carl WETZ and wife, nee WAHL of near Bracken, died of pneumonia on Oct. 22 at Camp Lee, Virginia, where he was attending a government veterinary school. Deceased was born and raised at Bracken and has attained the age of twenty-nine years and three months. He was inducted into army service in June 1918 and after being stationed at Camp Travis about three weeks, he was sent to Camp Lee where his untimely death occurred. His parents, upon being informed of his sickness, journeyed to Camp Lee hoping to be with their son in his precarious condition, but he had succumbed before they reached him. The body was shipped here and reached Bracken October 28th from which interment was held at the Bracken Cemetery.

Eventually, the family had his body moved to Zion Cemetery in Schertz next to the graves of his parents Carl and Emma WETZ. The graves are located today at FM 1103 and Chelsea Drive.

On November 16, 1918 news came that the Kaiser had abdicated, and an armistice had been signed by Germany. Peace was being discussed. This made for the biggest demonstration ever held in Guadalupe County. Every church bell in every community rang, and the noise mounted with horns, firecrackers, shotguns, and anything that could make noise joined in.

The *Seguin Enterprise* reported all stores were closed, and funeral notices appeared announcing the death of Kaiser WILHELM with a funeral to take place at 3:00 o'clock in the afternoon at the courthouse yard. School children met at the high school and marched in a parade followed by autos and people marching and waving flags. A group left Seguin and went to New Braunfels to use their artillery there.

Neighboring Comal County also celebrated and recorded that it had oversubscribed its quota to each Liberty Loan Drive during the war and furnished some 500 young men for the Expeditionary Force. Like Cibolo and Schertz, Comal County had participated in rationing and doing everything for the war effort.

Cibolo and Schertz were not as organized as Seguin, but the effect was the same as citizens stood in front of their homes or rode to tell neighbors who might not know what had happened. An effigy of the Kaiser was hung in Seguin from a scaffold and later buried. It wasn't recorded that something as dramatic happened in Cibolo and Schertz, but all communities spent the day talking of the peace and end of the war.

Under presidential warrants 6,300 German-Americans were arrested during the war. Most were paroled although 2,300 were jailed at some point. More than 2,000 indictments in the U.S. came about because of the Espionage Act.

Cibolo and Schertz had survived during the difficult times of World War I because they quietly continued to be proud American citizens. It is a compliment to their fortitude and loyalty.

When the War ended in 1918, the flu epidemic in the same year left a number of casualties in Cibolo as in all parts of the world. Burial in St Paul's Cemetery in 1917 and 1918 included members of the BOETTING, BRINKOETER, PFANNSTEIL, RITTIMAN, ELAM, and KRUEGER families who likely suffered from some consequences of the flu.

Bank Robbery in New Braunfels

Biggest news in 1922 was the robbery of the New Braunfels State Bank by the NEWTON BOYS gang. During the lunch hour on March 10th the gang entered the bank with weapons, threatened the president and four employees, scooped up money and bonds, and left. They drove toward the Cibolo Creek where they waited the rest of the day and night in a brushy area hidden from view, and then made their way to San Antonio. A year before this, they had robbed the Boerne State Bank and a month later robbed two banks in the same night at Hondo. It was a time when small banks were nervous and willing to put on extra help to guard at night, but if the NEWTON BOYS were now making robberies in the daytime, the scene was different. The gang seemed particularly interested in banks that had safes with square doors that could be blown off with nitroglycerin. It was the topic of all conversations for days after.

ENTERTAINMENT

For a good time, people of the area could go to Crescent Bend Dancehall on the Cibolo Creek. Bands from Austin and other cities came to play including the Steve Gardner Band. Mr. Gardner could play two clarinets at the same time, so audiences were delighted. There was also Louie's Little German Band led by Louis Scheel with Wallace Biesenbach as one of his band members. Eddie STAPPER built the dancehall about 1926, but ownership changed several times to include Emil WIEDERSTEIN and Ewald PFEIL. A later owner, Emil KOPPLIN, awoke to find that Cibolo Creek had flooded the place during the night, and he could have drowned in his own dance hall. For anyone during Prohibition who wanted to imbibe, at least four known bootleggers operated in the area.

Groups who did not want to go to the dancehall could entertain themselves with various kinds of parties. A "play-party" was very close to a dance but not called that. An "apron party" was one where boys had to hem aprons brought by girls. There were "storm parties" which were surprise parties. A box supper called for food to be prepared by a young lady, and her offering was bid upon by the young men. The German families particularly liked target shooting and were quite accomplished in that. Plus, there were always quilting, possum hunts, or musical evenings.

1941-PRESENT

It was:

The center of Cibolo volunteers.

The location of joy and laughter.

The place for knowledge.

The heart of a community.

THE GRANGE ON MAIN STREET, CIBOLO, TEXAS

"Grange" is defined as a farm or area surrounding a farm, but it became more in 1867 when the Patrons of Husbandry, or The Grange, was founded to advance methods of agriculture as well as promote social and economic needs of the rural communities of the United States. A surge in membership was notable in Iowa, Minnesota, Wisconsin, and Illinois as areas enjoyed educational and social activities. Also, it was the first time that smaller communities felt they were having an effect on political issues as they sent their recommendations to state and federal officials.

The formative years in Texas were 1873-1875 when people were very interested in organizing a Texas State Grange and met in Austin in 1874 with 121 members present representing sixty-two subordinate groups. It was a time for rural areas to speak their minds, and it was an enthusiastic response to the call to join a Grange movement. The first State Master or president was Col. J.B. JOHNSTON of Freestone County. By 1875 when the second convention was held in Dallas, some of the earlier glow had worn off. A high at one point of over 40,000 had diminished to a little over half that number. Apathy was the word used by some of the officers, but they still made resolutions saying that financial aids without effort of self-help would hurt the government, and convict labor should not be used on cotton farms. One officer of the State Grange stated he had traveled 2,885 miles by horse and buggy and public conveyance to visit Granges all over Texas. Talk was important as the areas shared their concerns to visit Granges.

There was an up and down cycle of weather and the economy for the next two years had a definite influence on Grange membership, but the need was still strongly supported in newspaper editorials. Grange members were aware that agriculture was being ignored in some universities, and they knew there was a specific need for it. In 1880 the State Master gave harsh criticism to the A & M college in Bryan because he believed the school had not met hopes by many farmers of having young men thoroughly trained in the science and practice of agriculture. He noted that (1) the curriculum was not really an agriculture curriculum (why was Latin in the mix?) (2) there was wretched mismanagement of the institution of A & M (3) no professor of agriculture was employed full time (4) there was overcrowded study rooms (5) the water supply came from a nearby pond (6) the sinks were not healthy and should be removed and replaced (7) even the bathrooms needed dramatic improvements. It was altogether an uninviting situation for those who wanted to study agriculture.

Membership in the Grange continued to decline sharply to a figure just over 4,300, but the severe drought could be blamed since many farmers were forced to go out of business. The topic of education continued to be on the Grange agenda when in 1896 the State Master remarked that some female teachers were only filling time in the classroom until favorable matrimonial prospects came about, and male teachers often taught only so they would have enough money to go into another business.

Cibolo had developed by the turn of the century into a strong agricultural center for raising animals and food products. The population was small although there was a Main Street with a few businesses. The coming of the Galveston, Harrisburg, and San Antonio Railroad in 1877 had given the town a way to ship items to other cities. More than 455 farms existed between Marion to Selma and Cibolo Creek. San Antonio was close enough to make a living in Cibolo a pleasant existence.

On February 6, 1941, a group of Cibolo farmers and businessmen gathered at the Cibolo school building to discuss the organization of a chapter of the National Grange. Grange members from Elmendorf and Converse were guests, and they told of the benefits that could be had from having a Grange chapter in Cibolo. It would be a way to consolidate community activities and present aid to worthwhile projects. It meant a voice to politicians letting them know what people were feeling. State officials were also on hand to discuss the service that a Grange could do for citizens. Helmuth DIETZ was elected temporary chairman and Alfred SCHRAUB temporary secretary.

At the second meeting on February 13, 1941, the group received encouragement from the Guadalupe County Agent who recognized what a value the organization could be for Cibolo. Officers were elected:

>Master: John MURPHY
>Secretary: Mrs. Elaine SCHLATHER
>Lecturer: Ray O'BRYANT
>Overseer: Eugene TSCHOEPE
>Treasurer: Ed STOLTE
>Chaplain: Hugo SCHNEIDER
>Steward: Alfred SCHRAUBB
>Assistant Steward: Franklin STOLTE
>Lady Assistant Steward: Mrs. Helmuth DIETZ
>Ceres: Mrs. Ewald PFIEL
>Flora: Mrs. John MURPHY
>Pomona: Mrs. Carl MOTSCH

An executive committee was made up of R.E. TURNAGE, Tommy MEEK, and Walter HILD.

A list of charter members was not recorded, but an incomplete list from later documents included the following names who were not officers:

    Millie ACKERMANN
    Milton ACKERMANN
    Agnes BIEGERT
    Ottmar DIETZ
    Mrs. Ottmar DIETZ
    Linda HILD
    Alwin LIECK
    Mrs. Ray O'BRYANT
    Anton PFEIL
    Ewald PFIEL
    Mrs. Emil RANE
    Otto RANE
    Mrs. Otto RANE
    George SCHLATHER
    Elmer SCHLATHER
    Ernst SCHLATHER
    Mrs. Alfred SCHRAUB
    Hilmar STAPPER
    Mrs. Hilmar STAPPER
    Mrs. Hugo SCHNEIDER

During this time, at least fifty-six charter members were later recorded, but it is likely the figure is much higher. On February 20, 1941, there were ninety-seven members who attended a meeting at the school, and most of them if not all could have been charter members. This was the second largest charter membership group in Texas Grange history. Immediately, the Grange began to help with the needs of the community by participating in 4-H shows, sponsoring needy youth, doing any activity that would help the more than 300 residents of Cibolo.

Meeting at the school was the only option for the membership for the rest of 1941 as World War II began. In March of 1942 Master John MURPHY was forced to resign because of health reasons, and Eugene TSCHOEPE was elected to the position of Master.

A new meeting place was leased in 1942 when the Grange began meeting at the Crescent Bend Dancehall on Cibolo Creek. Eddie STAPPER built the hall about 1926, but ownership changed several times to include Emil WIEDERSTEIN and Ewald PFEIL. The hall survived the flooding of Cibolo Creek and Prohibition; it was the best that could be found for a meeting place for a large group such as the Grange.

There was a family atmosphere about the place as people came to relax and listen to music. It was also a place that the Grange could use for fund raising dances, and there was a need for revenue if they were to help their neighbors in wartime.

Sponsorship of 4-H, workshops, discussion of good soil conservation, blood drives, collections for the war effort as well as socials were held. In 1944, Hugo SCHNEIDER was elected Master and held a successful membership drive.

In 1946, a new Master, Oscar KRAMER, encouraged the organization of a Junior Grange which would meet at the school building. At that time, twenty-one young people formed a Junior Grange to include the following names: STAPPER, HILDEBRAND, KOEHLER, BIESENBACK, TOLLE, SASSMAN, SCHNEIDER, LAMBRECHT, and ZIMMERMANN. They elected their Junior Master as Lawrence SCHNEIDER and focused on educational programs such as learning new crafts. The National Master visited to see how the thriving Junior Grange was doing, and complimented the group on their busy schedule of helping the community as well as having a good time.

At this point in 1947, Grange members agreed a building committee should be appointed for a permanent structure on Main Street of Cibolo. It was the perfect place to be seen and to do activities for the community. The first-ever fundraising sausage supper and dance was held for the benefit of the building fund. Slowly the amount grew, and Mr. and Mrs. Ernst SCHLATHER donated an acre of land for the location.

One year from the time a committee was appointed, a building was obtained. Master Otto

KOEHLER presided over the war surplus building that had been an officer's mess hall at the World War II Army base, Camp Swift, in Bastrop. The base had seen a population come and go, reaching as many as 50,000 including German POWs whose job was to spend their days stuffing olives for the nearby farmers who needed help. Many complained that the job was too easy for captured soldiers, but the farmers intervened.

By 1947, only about 800 personnel were still at Camp Swift, and the purchase of a building was a welcome transaction. The building came to Cibolo in two sections, and members used many volunteer hours to put the sections back together and to devise plumbing and electricity. It would be called the Cibolo Community Hall and be a place for any activities that Cibolo residents might need. The first official meeting was held on August 11, 1948 with a full house in attendance. The Grange and the people of Cibolo now had a home.

Charles DENNIS became the new Master in 1949, and it was a busy time of helping those in Cibolo with the projects for business and agriculture, young and old. The Grange sponsored monthly fifteen-minute safety programs broadcast on Radio Station KWED in Seguin, and for the next two years its members participated in 4-H shows and kept the Cibolo Community hall in good working condition. There are no records of specific projects during this time, but it can be said that there were numbers of them as in later years.

The year 1952 was proclaimed a banner year, Charles FLING became Master and helped direct the community service events that accounted for more than 800 hours of volunteer work. The Grange offered a place for blood drives, collections of gifts to charitable organizations such as the American Cancer Society, Boy Scouts and 4-H meetings, and they decorated a float for the July 4th parade in Seguin. There were programs on soil conservation practices, collection of scrap iron (895 pounds), and the donation of two registered pigs to two 4-H boys who had applied for them.

One Grange member, Richard TOLLE, reported his best crop in twenty-one years on a one-hundred-acre farm, and the Grange members believed they were sharing information that would help them all. With so many groups and families using the building, it was always in need of repair and upkeep. Grange members always answered the call for work days. At the state Grange convention in Hamilton, Charles DENNIS of Cibolo served on the Executive Committee, and many Cibolo Grangers attended.

The fifteen-minute radio scripts on KWED continued in 1952 with emphasis on striping safety lines across highways and educating the community on the need for school safety signs. Also, the Grange posted signs in grocery stores to warn of danger in some grocery carts which could tip and produce accidents for young children. Parallel parking spots were marked on Main Street in the business district. Legislation was addressed as it was every month by sending letters lobbying for a Farm-To-Market road from Cibolo to the San Antonio-Austin Highway.

A discussion of a need for entertainment for Cibolo's younger members led to the organizing of the Young People's Community Association that started with twenty members. Officers included: President, George SASSMAN; Vice President, Vernelle TOLLE; Secretary, Darlene TOLLE; Treasurer, Frances STAPPER. The Grange helped the group by sponsoring volleyball, table tennis, bunco, and a mock criminal trial at the monthly meetings.

In 1952, there was a continued emphasis on community beautification. The environment was very important to those who lived in Cibolo. Also, the need for training in first aid was evident, so several programs were given to help Grange members and anyone else who wanted to learn more. Instruction in prevention of boll weevils was of particular interest to farmers who had to deal with the problem as they produced their crops. Soul and Soil Sunday was a time for the Grange to be present as a group at a certain church in the community, and a number of members were recognized at services. Radio scripts continued to be aired, and more than 862 hours of volunteer service were recorded by Grange members on a number of projects.

"One night during the cold winter the rural telephone began to ring. Six Grange members and their families answered the call to help fight the fire which was burning one of the larger farm barns in the community."

This was a description of the evening when the large fire began and was contained to the barn. Lives were saved, but Grange members began to discuss what Cibolo would need to do to have a volunteer fire department. It would take many meetings, fund raisers, planning, and commitments. The Grange was willing to be the leader and do what had to be done.

Moving the Grange from Camp Swift in Bastrop to Cibolo 1947. Photo courtesy of Mrs. George Sassmann.

All those long hours of volunteering were recognized by the Texas Grange as Cibolo won the top honor in the 1952 Community Service Contest. Master Charles FLING had guided the various committees and identified community needs. At the state convention in Hamilton the trouble spots in the world were identified as Korea, Iran, Egypt, and Greece, and the convention and its members called for a great leader to step out of the ranks in Washington to lead the United States back to "safety and sanity." The 2,366 State Grange members resolved to offer a course in first aid for any emergency atomic bomb blast.

The State Grange discouraged travel and very large gatherings in reaction to the polio situation which was more evident in summer months and hot weather. Suggestions included using funds for Farm-To-Market Roads rather than super highways.

The Cibolo Grange continued in its accumulation of volunteer hours, now more than 3000 in 1953. The members gave unselfishly to the March of Dimes, youth leadership, state, and local programs for the deaf, 4-H, local nursing and rehab centers, and other organizations.

With the population of Cibolo only slightly more than 350, it was amazing that the Grange membership was 149. E.K. RICHARDS took as many pictures as possible of people using the Grange Hall, but it was a daunting task because of the numbers.

Master Elmo RUST encouraged the Grange to sponsor the Cibolo Community Fair on August 12th, a first for them and a large project, but it was well attended. "Old-fashioned" was the key description with displays of items made by hand and of animals and farm products.

At the request of music lovers, a Cibolo Grange Band was formed and appeared at dances, reunions, and the State Grange convention. Band members were Henry SCHRAUB, Herbert KRICKHAHN, Charles FLING, Edgar BRAHM, Mrs. Henry SCHRAUB, Mrs. Edgar VORDENBAUM, Emil WIEDERSTEIN, and Andrew TOLLE. The group was received and asked to play as many times as they could put the event in their schedules.

Since the hall was the hub of activities for Cibolo, Grange members used it for bingo to benefit Boy Scouts, held programs on soil conservation, improved the hall when necessary, and held a sausage supper that netted $147.88. The supper was a success with plans for it to be an annual event.

Hugo SCHNEIDER was chairman of the Cibolo Community Fair Committee and organized the dance that was held after the day's activities. Exhibits at the Fair included livestock, swine, poultry, rabbits, pigeons, field crops, handiwork, clothing, baked food, canned food, vegetables, arts and crafts, and community booths for any business or church. Baked goods division included quick breads, chiffon cakes, macaroons, bread, biscuits, apple pie, angel food cake, butter cake, and coffee cake. Rules for the State Grange Cake Baking Contest indicated a division for un-iced chocolate chiffon cake baked in a nine-inch pan, permission to use a Better Crocker recipe, a copy of the recipe, and membership in the Grange as the prerequisite for the entry.

Though membership at this time was about 148, only about a third of that number was active volunteers for community events. Blood donations, Red Cross, 4-H, the popular sausage supper, and a new tamale supper were a few of the events. Since the Community Fair had been free with no admission charge, it took a number of committees to organize the 300 entries.

Thirty members of the Grange came to put a new roof on the Hall, and some said that the oldest member of the Grange was the first to step on the ladder. It was easy to see how so many volunteer hours were accumulated.

The State Grange Convention attendees were shocked the federal government's administration had requested an increase in the national debt to 290 billion dollars. They also didn't like the fact that the Korean War had been called a "police action" and did not want to be involved in a major conflict.

Congress, they stated in a resolution, should examine the structure of the State Department. It had been a hard year for farmers with little or no rain across the state of Texas for almost two years. Water conservation was a topic of interest for everyone, farmer and non-farmer alike.

Cibolo's Grange continued to support the Grange Creed: "We desire a proper equality, equity, and fairness; protection for the weak, restraint upon the strong, in short, justly distributed burdens and justly distributed power."

Cibolo took first place in the State Grange Community Service Contest and placed in the top ten in the National Grange Community Service Contest with a $1000 prize award. A total of 4,542 Granges entered nationwide. Cibolo marked their win because of thousands of volunteer hours.

The development of a Volunteer Fire Department had been in their minds for more than five years. Cibolo had approximately 500 families. With no fire protection in the area, the Grange worked steadily toward their goal of a Volunteer Fire Department until their total funding was $4000. Over $2000 had been raised by the Grange; other donations came from corporate sponsors and donations. The number of volunteer hours on this project came to 2000. Official organization was made in March 1956 with an eleven-member board of directors.

Suppers at one dollar a plate had been the earliest fund raisers with a tradition of the same sausage recipe made each year with a recipe handed down to the head cook. The sausage supper became associated with the fire department. It was a two to three-day event: grinding meat, preparing sausage casings, mixing, seasoning, smoking meat, chilling it overnight, and then keeping an iron kettle going over an open fire.

The first truck purchased was a 1956 Ford two-ton chassis. This was only a beginning in establishing a functioning Volunteer Fire Company. Later, one hundred families pledged enough support to buy a 500 – 600 pumper that could be put on the chassis.

On Christmas Eve 1956, Grange members and non-members who were volunteer firemen, dug trenches for the concrete foundation for a fire house. Unless the trenches were done at this time, the donated concrete could not be used for free because of tax considerations. The Cibolo Grange and Cibolo men and women did what they had always done; they worked for a community cause.

Membership was steady in 1957 with over 163 members and an accumulation of volunteer hours as high as in 1956. Because of their many completed projects, the Cibolo Grange once again won first place in the Texas Grange Community Service Contest. There were first aid classes, clothing donations for Boysville, dog vaccinations, and the completed fire equipment necessary for the fire truck to work properly. Their hours added up as they dug the trenches for the fire department, leveled the cement, polished floors, and set tile on weekends and after their own work hours.

Weather had been unusually dry for several seasons, but the Grange still supported the 1957 Community Fair to show farmers were still producing in difficult times. It was said to be an excellent attendance for the August celebration. There were commercial booths for the following:

Charles DENNIS returned as Master in 1957 and continued at the post for the next two years. Once more, the Cibolo Grange aided the Volunteer

Fire Department with a gift of $1,911.10, held a dog vaccination, planted trees, had programs on soil and water conservation, repaired road hazards on community roads where trees had blocked views, held a Community Fair, chaperoned one night a week at the Cibolo Bowling Club for youth, and continued to send resolutions and recommendations to state and federal officials on a variety of topics. The Grange worked carefully with the FFA to handle a rat and mouse migration and infestation by selling poisons which would be effective but not harmful to the environment.

Since the area around Cibolo Grange was unincorporated, there was no means of taxation, so the Grange took on as much responsibility as possible for the safety and wellbeing of over 500 families who now lived within the area. Their yearly sausage supper sold 850 plates, the money going for a variety of causes. Mrs. Benno STAPPER was named state Conservation Homemaker of the year, and the Grange honored her for the award.

Since the Community hall was used for numerous events, there were things done each year to maintain and improve its condition: re-doing the floors (sanding, varnishing, waxing), putting in new drapes, installing new indoor lights. There was a variety of things to do most of the time, and Grangers never asked for a rest. Because of all the efforts in 1957, the Cibolo Grange once again earned a first place among all Texas Granges in the State

Community Service Contest.

Putting together a Cibolo Community Fair every year was not an easy task for the Grange, and in 1958 they worked especially hard. They involved: 44 committees, 202 people, and 1500 volunteer hours.

Charles ORTH won first place for molasses. The State Grange awarded Cibolo an honorable mention for Community Service for 1958.

Dog vaccinations were important to the Cibolo people and had been for several years, and 1959 was no different. They were inexpensive, handled by a veterinarian, and were at a convenient place for owners to bring their pets. More than 198 dogs were vaccinated in Cibolo and Marion. Aid to the Volunteer Fire Department continued because it was so vital to the community. Also, the Grange showed educational films at the hall, supervised special youth programs in which seven young boys each planted an acre of farmland and competed for the best yield and an eight-dollar first place prize, held the Community Fair, cooked a sausage supper, donated to the school to encourage education of Cibolo children, and made three new town markers to show travelers where the town was located. There were more than 2,500 volunteer hours recorded with over $2000 in the Grange treasury to donate for worthy causes.

Of all the scrapbooks made for the Cibolo Grange through the years, the one for 1960 was only one of two made with wood. There is no name to say who took the time to use that material and etch the year and name on the outside, but it is beautiful and is still kept at the Cibolo Grange today. The Cibolo Grange membership numbered a high of 185 with a good raise in the number who participated on a regular basis to ninety. Hugo SCHNEIDER directed programs on agricultural aid to farmers, highway safety, dog vaccinations (146 in Cibolo and Marion), public relations, help for the Volunteer Fire Department, 4-H, Boy Scouts, Red Cross, March of Dimes, local charities, and at least twenty projects in all.

David ARTZ had already had five surgeries and would need more, so the Grange helped with another supper serving their famous sausage, peas, potato salad, and a dessert. Bad weather threatened their festivities, but 800 people came and ate or bought plates to take home. The sausage supper raised $2,465 for the boy and his family. Every item for the supper was donated.

A traditional sausage supper was served again in support of the Fire Department. Again, an outpouring of 1000 people ate or bought plates to take home, bringing in a total of $1000 after any expenses.

The Grange held a barbecue chicken supper, and it was a big success, so there was discussion of making it an annual event. There was also a Rural Life Sunday with visits to area churches in groups.

A difficult project taken on by the Grange was helping in the construction of a new water reservoir for additional water storage. It meant 120,000 gallons of water for Cibolo, and it took more than 720 volunteer hours with 90 percent of the membership helping at one time or in some way. Because of this and other actions taken by the Grange, Cibolo Grange received first place in the State Community Service Contest.

The youth were not forgotten with several activities for them. Over 3,500 volunteer hours were reported as Grangers worked on community projects for all ages. Leona DREYER won an essay contest on highway safety, and scored high at the state level. Mrs. Richard TOLLE was the top homemaker in the county and region. The Cancer Society, San Antonio State Hospital, March of Dimes, 4-H also received donations. And bingo—there was always time for fun.

This period from 1950 to 1960 marked an amazing time for the Cibolo Grange as their community service had been recognized as first place five times, second place twice, and third place and honorable mention three times. It was fifth at the National Grange level twice. All the recognition showed the determination and dedication of Cibolo's people.

The next six years are not documented with scrapbooks or records for some reason, or they have been lost or misplaced through time. But it is certain that Cibolo Grange continued in their service to their community through every available means.

Charles FLING returned as Master in 1961-1962. In February 1966, the Cibolo Grange celebrated its Silver Anniversary with more than 130 members who were still living and able to attend the event. Each were given a lapel decoration of wheat tied with royal blue and gold ribbon, symbolic of the Grange.

Also, in 1966, the Cibolo Grange had state winners in the sewing contests. Mrs. Atlee KREBS and daughter, Ella, took first places. The Grange projected the idea that sewing "develops an understanding of self in order that one may select and make clothing which is becoming and expressive of personality." There were always games and suppers, safety demonstration, clothing drives for Boysville, support for children in orphanages, aid to the volunteer fire department, help for any who needed it, and an awareness that the community was important to everyone.

A chili supper in 1967 raised $117.91 for educational films. Overseer Fred WIEDNER coordinated an emphasis on 4-H, Girl Scouts, Boy Scouts, youth camps, and health needs. Several donations to schools gave educational encouragement. It was typical at any Grange meeting to bring up a resolution on some state or federal action, discuss it, and in later meetings develop it into a letter to officials. Response from those officials in the form of a letter was always noted and preserved.

Booster Night in 1968 drew seventy people in attendance with forty-five Grange members. Helmuth DREYER was honored for his five years of service as Master, and Elmo RUST for his duties in that position for the second time. Cibolo winners in the State Youth Grange contests were for photo, baking, crafts, and needlework. Mrs. Alma ROSENBAUM was recognized because she had only missed fourteen meetings in the past twenty-seven years as a member. Bermuda grass seed was sent to an orphanage in Vietnam where Larry GEMBLER, a Grange member, was working in the Navy. The playground at the orphanage was in dire need of grass and this gift would help. There were always contributions to 4-H, Boy Scouts, and a Cibolo Community Fair.

Social security was a serious subject where monthly payments were being increased from $44 to $55, so resolutions were made, and letters sent to Washington. Voter registration was emphasized as the Grange continued informative programs on three radio stations, releases in six newspapers, and several local discussions with various groups. Of course, there was time for a barbecue chicken supper which the community really liked, bingo, and game nights. One song that became a favorite and sung many nights in the hall was the tune of "My Bonnie Lies Over the Ocean."

Lyrics:
>My Bonnie lies over the ocean
>My Bonnie lies over the sea
>My Bonnie lies over the ocean
>Oh, bring back my Bonnie to me.
>
>My mother's an apple pie maker
>My father fiddles for tin.
>My sister scrubs for a living.
>Oh boy, how the money rolls in.
>Rolls in, Rolls in
>Oh boy, how the money rolls in.

Chorus:
>Bring back, bring back,
>Oh, bring back my Bonnie to me, to me.
>Bring back, bring back,
>Oh, bring back my Bonnie to me.

There was another gap in scrapbooks from 1969-1972, but 1972 continued the active life that was the Cibolo Grange. Meet the Candidates Night, Booster Night, Public School Week, support for 4-H and FFA, dog vaccinations (125 animals), voter registration, cakes and cookies for servicemen, a volleyball tournament, aid to the Volunteer Fire Department, community hall changes and upkeep, eyeglasses for children who could not afford them—was an outstanding list of things done. Officers leading the Cibolo Grange at this point included:

> Master: Elmo RUST
> Overseer: Fred WIEDNER
> Lecturer: Clarence PROPHET
> Steward: Monroe ZUHEL
> Assistant Steward: Marvin POHMIYER

"Trash to Treasure" sales amounted to $350 while a spaghetti and meatball meal gave support to the Vocational Ag Department at Samuel Clemens High School with Vocational Ag teacher Toby CONNER helping in the plan. Education about the voter registration system explained that registration had to be fifty days before the election. Re-districting was discussed as an important problem as well as voluntary prayer in school, so both petitions were sent to Austin and Washington. The first permanent road signs, 500 in number, were placed in the county so that emergency personnel could find locations of various homes.

A new attraction at the Guadalupe County Fair was a Bake Off, and Grange member, Mrs. Leroy SCHEILE won second place and a $12 cash prize for her pecan slices. The recipe was the only one given in all the Grange scrapbooks.

Pecan Slices

2 eggs
1 cup brown sugar
1 cup white sugar
¾ cup melted margarine
¼ cup sifted flour
1 cup chopped pecans
tsp. vanilla

Combine first four ingredients. Add flour, nuts, and vanilla. Place on a greased 9x9x2 inch pan and bake at 350 degrees for 35 minutes. Cut into bars while warm.

A special event took place in 1973 when the Cibolo Community Hall became the property of Cibolo Grange. A dissolution of the Cibolo Community Hall gave the assets of the Association, which was the hall, to the Cibolo Grange. It would still be a hall used by the community, but it would be totally maintained by the Grange. Continued support was given to safety programs, a volleyball tournament, Booster Night, cookies for servicemen, and fruitcake sales, something new which garnered $92.88. Crime Prevention was encouraged through the purchase of inscribing tools which could be checked out from the Grange to mark items which could be stolen. A goal of eighteen entries for the state sewing contest was met. At the yearly dog vaccinations, sixty-four dogs were vaccinated in Cibolo.

George and Ellise SASSMAN were recognized for years of service as managers of the Community Hall. Charles DENNIS, Martha DENNIS, and

Stella LIECK received pins for twenty-five years of membership.

Officers were the same for this year, but some had not been named in the previous scrapbook:

>Lady Assistant Steward: Marsha DREYER
>Chaplain: Richard TOLLE
>Secretary: Leona SCHNEIDER
>Gatekeeper: Charles ORTH
>Ceres: Rena DRYER
>Pomona: Helen TOLLE
>Flora: Louise WIEDNER

Once again, Cibolo Grange took first place in the State Community Service Program receiving a $100 savings bond.

Over 3,800 service hours to the community were given in 1974, and Cibolo Grange used on many occasions the building now called Grange Hall. Once again there were pet vaccinations (112 in Cibolo), bake sales, Community Night, programs on subjects of interest to the members and non-members, clothing and food for needy families, eyeglasses for those who could not afford them, recycling of newspapers and aluminum cans, paint for the Grange hall, volleyball tournaments, yearly support for the Volunteer Fire Department with the widely-attended barbecue chicken and sausage suppers. Membership was beginning to drop in numbers. Still, those who stayed continued to work hard.

Community Night in 1975 brought sixty-two people. During the year, forty-six people were busy and glad to help. Bennie BOCK II, state representative from Guadalupe County, paid a visit to the Grange hall as the discussion was about current farm policies. Help for Christian Corral, a home for children who were without parental care, had been going on for several years and continued this year with a Christmas party for the children. Discussion of the ERA was spirited. What did it mean? Would eighteen-year-old girls be required to register for the draft? Grange members exchanged questions and concerns trying to gain information before sending any resolutions to Austin and Washington.

No scrapbook for 1976 and some thought 1977 was a quiet year with no major projects. There were, however, any number of activities. A bake sale supported youth going to state convention, a Christmas program for the community as well as the Christian Corral children. Support for the usual activities in the past continued.

Even if membership was beginning to dwindle, volunteer hours accumulated as Grange members refurnished the Grange Hall, helped local families, and held Meet the Candidates Night. Of special concern was traffic sign vandalism, so Cibolo Grange conducted programs and wrote radio scripts for broadcast about the danger of such destruction. Over 800 hours were served to benefit the community.

A new Master, Lester GERLOFF, was elected in 1979, and it was another year with no major projects. They continued to support the pet vaccinations, youth programs, recycling of newspapers and aluminum cans, baking contest, and the Volunteer Fire Department through sausage suppers and barbecue chicken suppers.

In 1980 a change with a new Master came when Ethel POHMIYER took the helm and held it for the next five years. The membership who had been active decreased to fewer than 40 because of ill health, but the number never seemed to keep Grange members from their goals. They continued with the same programs with less personnel. To the delight of all, the suppers, food, and game nights continued.

Membership in 1981 was still at forty, but they continued as though there were many more. Then on February 13, 1981, the Cibolo Grange celebrated its 40th anniversary with six former masters able to attend. There were displays and decorations that certainly expressed the spirit of the anniversary. It was a special time bringing many visitors from all over the area. For more than 40 years, Grange members had volunteered thousands of hours, all for those who needed help.

The National Grange Master, Edward ANDERSON, spoke at a later visit and warned that new American President Ronald Reagan's farm policy could be too conservative with inadequate price supports. He noted that Grange membership had been declining in the past twenty years due to shrinking numbers of farm families. He did not oppose foreign ownership of farms despite concern from some conservative groups on the matter.

Since it was an anniversary year, the Cibolo Grange completed the usual number of projects with a goal to top the previous year. These efforts were rewarded with a third-place state award for Community Service.

Improvements for the Grange hall was a priority in 1982 with a thorough inspection to find trouble spots. There was a need for new windows, doors, and steps. At least thirty-four members helped with the installation and repairs. The chicken barbecue meant cooking seventy-five whole fryers, a number agreed upon to be manageable, plus all the extras: potato salad, vegetables, and cakes. The price remained reasonable, $3 per large plate and $2 per small one. The result was $377.80 to be used for Grange charities. There was also the annual sausage supper to benefit the Volunteer Fire Department. Newspaper ads announced aluminum can collections, programs on various topics including organic gardening, an active youth program, and pet vaccinations (316 in Cibolo and Marion). The Grange hall became a polling place for county voters. At the State Grange Convention Cibolo received third place in Community Service and first place for a Harvest Display that featured plants and colors of the area.

Continued support for deaf programs in the area and the state were evident in 1983. After fifteen years, Leona SCHNEIDER retired as Grange secretary; a reception honored her. The pet vaccination continued to be popular with 136 animals in Cibolo and 157 in Marion being vaccinated. Food—now that was always a part of Grange activities with the chicken barbecue plates selling very quickly and the sausage supper well attended. More than thirty members were able to help, but the problem of aging members was certainly a subject that was discussed. Home Demonstration Agent, Tabbie GRIFFIN, gave several programs and information on snack foods and better health. Preliminary work on the Community Neighborhood Crime Watch began. For the solid program that Cibolo Grange presented, they were honored with fourth place in the State Community Service awards.

Master Ethel POHMIYER worked with committees to coordinate efforts for a Community Neighborhood Crime Watch in 1984. Almost fifty Grange members helped to obtain the necessary $150 for signs and information to the public through radio broadcasts and newspaper articles. Attendance at many meetings in Cibolo and Marion and a general awareness of what the Crime Watch meant resulted in an emphasis of neighbor helping neighbor. The best locks for use in homes were on display. Because of this major project plus all the ones developed and carried out each year, Cibolo Grange received first place in the Community Service Award at the state convention.

When it came time to barbecue chickens the last Sunday in October, the Grange members decided to go all out—200 chickens. There was no problem selling the food, and the profit came to over $400 after the 115 hours of volunteering. Money could be used for familiar projects such as the American Cancer Society, Christian Corral Children's Home in New Braunfels, 4-H, programs for the deaf, nursing home refreshments, and scouting. Contests were entered in photography, cooking, and sewing. Total volunteer hours by Grange members were counted at 1,236. The National Grange Convention was in San Antonio, so several members attended. Keeping up the Grange hall was important because it was used for family reunions, parties, showers, weddings, and a polling place for elections.

A candidate forum in 1985 helped the community meet those running for office. Completion of a wheel chair ramp at Grange hall was important and necessary. There was also a first in baking at the State Convention in "men's forgotten cookies"—the definition of that was not given. Familiar things were done: help for the deaf, glasses for those unable to pay, the annual barbecue chicken dinner, provisions for the Christian Corral

Children's Home, collection of newspaper and aluminum cans, and bake sales. For more than ten years Cibolo Grange had supported the Volunteer Fire Department and worked on the firehouse as well. Pet vaccinations never slowed: 146 in Cibolo, 159 in Marion. Almost 1000 hours of volunteer service were recorded.

At the Sesquicentennial Celebration in Cibolo, the Grange participated by decorating a float. Repairs to the hall took some time, but not as much time as it had needed in some years. Barbecue chicken and sausage supper sales, as well as a bake sale came in at $900. Since barbecue had been so important to the Grange through the years, new pits were made of tanks which could handle many more numbers. Plate price increased slightly to $3.75 for a large plate, $3 for a small one. Mrs. TOLLE won first place for her quilt and Alma RUST was first in strawberry jam and placemats. A fourth place in Community Service for 1986 was given to Cibolo Grange.

A July 4th picnic was organized in 1987 for the first time and tickets for the event went fast with $140 worth in the first day of sales. Average attendance at meetings were usually twenty-five to thirty although special events drew more people. Needed repairs and maintenance for the hall were a constant: outside painting, new screen doors, and lights. Since it was always so time consuming to cook as many as they needed in previous years, Grangers decided 150 chickens would be enough—and sold out quickly. Pet vaccinations with Dr. WELLS numbered 284 in Cibolo and Marion. Because fund raising had gone so well, the Grange was able to support all the areas they had for so many years and not leave out one organization or cause. With the number of volunteer hours and a consistency of effort, the Cibolo Grange took first place in the State Community Service Awards.

A new project, a bike-a-thon, was developed in 1988 where youngsters got their bikes registered and participated in a rodeo. There was a youth bowling night, a pancake supper for EMS and the Volunteer Fire Department, educational programs, new chairs and tables for the Grange Hall, basic CPR training for those interested, and a Halloween party for children. All this and more designated the Cibolo Grange as fourth place in the State Community Service Awards. Pet vaccinations were now $4 with 300 animals in Cibolo and Marion receiving aid. With barbecued chickens, a carnival and a street dance, the result after paying expenses was $745 that went into the treasury.

The bike-a-thon had proved a success in the previous year, so it was continued in cooperation with the Cibolo Police Department. In 1989, a Junior Grange was re-organized, and the young Grangers were busy as they had fun but also helped every way they could. There was a spook house for the Halloween party, a complete rewiring of the Grange Hall, work on adding a storage room addition, and Christmas caroling. Barbecue chicken and a pancake breakfast brought food and community members to the hall with continuous volunteer hours to prepare the meals. The hall was used at no charge by 4-H and Cub Scouts, and for a nominal fee for parties, reunions, showers, and socials.

At the annual dog vaccination, the question of its origin of dog vaccinations came about, and the oldest Grange members reported that another Grange member had a pen of pigs attacked by a rabid dog in the early 1940s. Because of that, the need was shown, and an answer was given by Grange members. Three hundred dogs were vaccinated at Cibolo and Marion in 1989. Cibolo Grange received second place in Community Service Awards at the State Convention.

In 1990 at the State Convention, Elmo and Alma RUST were presented GRANGERS OF THE YEAR. Elmo was also given a memorial at the convention for his dedication and untiring devotion not only to the Cibolo Grange but to the State Grange as well. The Journal of Texas State Grange was dedicated to him. In Cibolo, trees were planted to honor his memory.

The State Grange opposed a state income tax, sent a recommendation to the legislature that it would be illegal for lawyers to advertise on television, drafted another resolution that would require those who were not citizens to be residents for twenty years before being eligible for benefits from the government. A great deal of discussion came about concerning all the recommendations. Master Arnold KATZER directed work in Cibolo on educational programs and encouraged the committees for the pancake breakfast, barbecue chicken supper, and a game night. The entire Grange hall was turned into a haunted house for Halloween to the delight of the community's children.

Fifty years—that's how long the Grange had been a presence in Cibolo, and a celebration was in order in 1991. Attending the event were seventy people who agreed that the use of the building had been truly important all these years. Fred WIEDNER was honored with a fifty-year membership pin. Abby WELLS, a junior Granger, won Best of Show at the National Grange Convention for her closeup color photos. The FFA at Samuel Clemens High School was given monetary support as were the Boy Scouts and Cub Scouts (thirty-two members). A tamale supper was added to the food events of barbecue chicken and a pancake breakfast. Twenty-four Grange members were active in the Volunteer Fire Department and were honored for their service. Pet vaccinations with Dr. Jake WELLS saw 158 in Cibolo and 156 in Marion.

In 1992, the treasury started the year with $3,226.49, a tribute to all the hard work by Grange members. An important project, and a first, was

Vial of Life, a uniform method of keeping medical information available. It would be stored in a vial that looked like a medication container and could be in a car's glove compartment and or in the upper right-hand shelf of a refrigerator. Each vial would include blood types, allergies, and current medication and would help medical personnel as they came to the aid of a person in medical distress. Family members would know where the Vial of Life was kept, and a note would be in a car. There were programs, demonstrations, and community information given out concerning the Vial of Life.

The Junior Grange held their own fund raisers that year which gave them $491.50 to give to Greater Randolph Area Christian Association Program, a food bank, and the assistance bureau for those in need in the nearby communities. The president of the Junior Grange was Tammy RAPPMUND. A wooden scrapbook for this period was only the second one of its kind made. The scrapbook gave recognition to Alma RUST for 248 volunteer hours, Wiley SANDERS for 170, and Horace SCOTT for 170. Dr. Jake WELLS, once again, headed the animal vaccination date and vaccinated 240 pets. Two senior citizen centers were furnished refreshments, and there was support for the local Hospice Agency in Seguin.

There was no scrapbook for 1993 and in 1994. The Grange felt there was no time for new major projects. There were now only thirty active members who barbecued chickens at the usual date of the fourth Sunday in October, held a garage sale, and emphasized family and community. Since the hall was used by so many groups, Master Cordell REINHARD oversaw the repairs such as repainting of the interior, new drapes, and floors replaced and refinished. Joining in with the work on a city drainage project added to the already mounting number of 340 hours spent on maintenance. The Grange hosted a Texas Grange leadership workshop, supported local libraries and area nursing homes, held programs on health care, protected the environment, and held a Community Christmas party. A possible veterans nursing home or rehabilitation center for Cibolo was discussed on several evenings.

At the State Convention of that year Leona SCHNEIDER and Fred WIEDNER were recognized as Golden Sheaf Members. Also, the State Grange passed resolutions in support of efforts to address skyrocketing costs of health care, to have the freedom to choose one's own doctor, and to make a reduction of the national debt. There was a recommendation which posted opposition to a federal police force. A National Grange first place winner in stuffed toys was Horace SCOTT. And all the efforts by Cibolo Grange gave them another first place in the State Community Service Awards.

Membership in 1995 was reduced to seventy-two overall with only twenty members producing volunteer hours. But the smaller group still emphasized recycling of newspapers and aluminum cans, worked with the Cibolo City Council, presented information to the community, supported Cub Scouts and 4-H, assisted the sick and elderly, held the annual pet vaccination, and barbecued chickens. The "magnificent twenty" accumulated 1800 volunteer hours, and because of their outstanding effort to continue all programs, they were awarded first place in the State Community Service Awards.

Another skip in scrapbooks put information to 1997 where a Friday Night Choir Club came into being with food and games for the youth as well as music. Help for Randolph Area Christian Assistance Program (RACAP) included a contribution to pay for electricity and 150 pairs of shoes for those who could not afford them. The Grange gave aid to deaf programs, Cub Scouts (sixty in membership), 4-H, demonstrations of water conservation, and information through radio interviews. Ross WELLS, son of Dr. Jake WELLS who had so ably handled dog vaccinations and a Grange member, received a $10,000 4-H scholarship. Pet vaccinations totaled 265 in Cibolo and Marion, and Alma RUST was first in state competition for muffins and cucumber pickles.

The 51st annual pet vaccination, dated back to 1947, now cost $5 in 1998, and there were 135 pets in Cibolo and 135 in Marion vaccinated. The "Hundred Year Flood" occurred the year before, so Cibolo was still recovering from the damage. Master Margaret POHMIYER made sure there was educational programs, a flea market sale, and help for 4-H, RACAP, Cub Scouts, local nursing homes, and a sausage supper, which had been an annual event since 1957. The Grange also helped with shut-ins, needy families, local and state deaf programs, and the repair of the strenuous projects. The rest of the forty members donated to projects. For Dairy Week, there was an ice cream social for the community and volunteers made refreshments for Pegasus Boarding Home, a rehab center.

Whatever else was happening in Cibolo, there always seemed to be interest in the Grange pet vaccination. In 1999, there were 134 in Cibolo, 100 in Marion. A new project was a gift and aid to the Christian Helping Center in Seguin where homeless were given meals and clothing. Stuffed teddy bears were presented to children in local hospitals.

Membership continued to decline although twenty participated in another new project, Threads of Love. This meant a monetary gift to purchase fabric to make gowns/blankets for premature newborns at local hospitals. There was a community Christmas party, help for shut-ins and needy families, support as always for the Volunteer Fire Department, and continual support for the 4-H, Cub Scouts, and Boy Scouts. Because such a small number were able to accomplish even new projects, Cibolo Grange was awarded third place in the State

Community Service Awards.

Beginning with the year 2000 and lasting until late 2012, the Cibolo Grange suffered from inactive membership. The problem had been coming for some time, but it surfaced completely at this point. Some members had moved away, some suffered health problems, and those left felt the responsibility of so much effort was more than they could handle monthly. There were some occasional actions such as a yard sale or ice cream social, and the hall rented for family reunions or gatherings, but the regular meetings were discontinued, dues were not paid, meetings were not recorded, and the State Grange designated Cibolo Grange as inactive.

It was a dramatic change in late 2012 when a group came together and set goals for the Cibolo Grange and the hall to become a center of community action. New officers were elected:

 Master/President: Lori WUEST
 Vice-President: Steven MUETH
 Treasurer: Lana GORALEWICZ
 Secretary: Dave WEAVER
 Chaplain: Maria ZAMORA
 Gatekeeper: Allen GORALEWICZ
 Steward: Juan SOLIS
 Lady Assistant Steward: Gerri MUETH
 Lecturer: Jessica SMITH
 Assistant Steward: Pat SOLIS
 Ceres: Cindy ROUSE

Pomona: Lilla GORALEWICZ
Flora: Terry GORALEWICZ
Executive Committee: Dave WEAVER, Juan SOLIS, Milton EDGE

The challenge had been met, and the hall once more was the scene of people and projects. Because of this, the State Grange re-instated Cibolo Grange as an active member in March 2013. Projects for the year were a community yard sale, support for Girl Scouts, a special needs social interaction for autistic young people. The members also sponsored Thanksgiving for the Troops, a pet vaccination, extensive hall renovations, a Farmers and Artisans Market held over a period of months, help for needy families, and perhaps the largest event in many years, host for Cibolo's National Night Out, which saw several hundred in attendance with information as well as refreshments. The year was a tremendous step for those Grange members who believed that volunteerism was alive and well in Cibolo.

Other Grange members who helped in the restoration of the building and its community outreach were Joshua WEAVER, Nathan MUETH, Kathryn MAHAN, and Hope and Jose TREVINO. It was not always easy, but the result was a building that once more echoed with voices.

So, what is the future of the Cibolo Grange? It looks like new faces and new strength will lift the beautiful record that the Grange had in the past and, once more, adhere to the principles of believing in their community. They've weathered through WWI, WWII, The Korean Conflict, the Cold War, and all sorts of technological advances. Cibolo itself has grown from that quiet little rural community to an incorporated town in 1965 to a bustling city of almost 25,000 by 2014. Growth in the area has been phenomenal, almost 715 percent since the beginnings of the Grange. There is always the question of whether people can be asked to give of themselves in a world that is changing faster than anyone can imagine. It has been done in the past as the Grange's record shows; it can be done in the future.

CIBOLO TEXAS • THE EARLY YEARS

EXCERPTS FROM NEWSPAPER ARTICLES

COURTESY OF JIM BURDETT
AND NEWSPAPERS.COM

This is only a sampling of articles gleaned from newspaper articles. It is our intention to show that although Cibolo may be a small town, many things have happened in and around the area.

Source: The Times (Shreveport, Louisiana. Fri, Jun 22, 1951

SUPERFORTRESS CRASH KILLS 3 IN TEXAS

Cibolo, Texas, June 21 (AP)—A B-29 Superfortress from Randolph field crashed and burned five miles northeast of here today and at least three men were killed.

Three others were seen parachuting from the plane before it crashed on a farm.

Wreckage of the plane was scattered over a 200-yard area.

The public relations officer at Randolph Field, San Antonio, said the plane was from there and that three bodies had been found in the wreckage.

A total of eight were believed to have been on the plane.

Source: Standard-Speaker (Hazleton, Pennsylvania)
Sat, Aug 1, 1992

SMALL PLANE CRASHES—

A biplane built in the 1930s crashed near Cibolo, Texas, after its propeller came off and sheared off the left wings, killing its pilot, authorities said.

Source: San Antonio Express (San Antonio, Texas)
Wed. Nov 25, 1970

AIRCRAFT FALLS IN RUGGED COUNTRY NORTHEAST OF S.A.

BY BOB DENMAN

Six persons died in a fiery crash of a single-engine about 10 miles north of Randolph AFB late Tuesday night. The plane crashed on the C.L. Honeycutt Ranch

about two miles northeast of Bracken in Southern Comal County, Bexar County sheriff's deputies said.

Source: The Seguin Gazette-Enterprise (Seguin, Texas)
Fri. Jun 14, 1985

PILOT, PASSENGER INJURED IN CRASH

BY MIKE BARBEE, STAFF WRITER

A twin-engine plane crashed at the New Braunfels Municipal Airport at about 1:45 p.m. Thursday. Plane owner John Thiel of Cibolo and passenger James Eichler of San Antonio were injured in the crash. The pilot of the twin-engine plane was trying a single-engine approach, officials said. They believe that Thiel and Eichler were on a training flight.

Cibolo Texas • The Early Years

Source: The Austin American (Austin, Texas) Wed. Jul 7, 1943

2 Randolph Fliers Die in Cibolo Crash

San Antonio, July 6 (UP)—The Randolph field public relations office Tuesday announced the deaths of 2nd LTs, Ward H. Moody and Harold P. Moore in an airplane crash near Cibolo. The accident occurred Monday.

Source: The Seguin Gazette-Enterprise (Seguin, Texas) Wed, Feb 10, 1982

Plane Hits Power Lines;
by Kathie Ninneman, Staff Writer

A small, single-engine plane crashed 400 yards short of the runway at Kardy's Airport Tuesday night killing the pilot and lone occupant, Arthur Franklin Bryson Jr., a Universal City Auto dealer.

Source: The Salina Journal (Salina, Kansas) Sun, Apr 23, 1978

Trains Collide—Cibolo, Texas (UPI)—Two Southern Pacific freight trains collided during a thunderstorm Saturday, causing a derailment, several injuries, a diesel spill and heavy damage to both trains.

Source: The Sedalia Democrat (Sedalia, Missouri) Tue, Oct 29, 1935

Cadet Dies in Plane Crash

Source: San Antonio, Texas, Oct 29 (AP)—The crash of an army plane today three miles northeast of Cibolo killed Flying Cadet Rhoe H. Harpis, 26, and injured Lieut. Walter S. Lee, 31, Randolph Field instructor. Randolph Field officers said the ship went into a spin.

Source: Lubbock Morning Avalanche (Lubbock, Texas)
Sat, Jul 25, 1931

FLIER UNINJURED

Source: San Antonio, Jul 24 (AP)—Lieut. Ralph P. Swofford, Kelly field student officer, escaped injury today when his pursuit plane struck telephone wires near Cibolo, causing the ship to crash to the ground. Although Lieut. Swofford was not hurt, his plane was reported considerably damaged.

Source: Fredericksburg Standard (Fredericksburg, Texas)
Fri, Aug 28, 1931

CIBOLO CITIZEN 100 YEARS OLD

Source: New Braunfels Tex., Aug 22—A large gathering of friends and relatives gathered at the home of Mrs. Antonia Keudell at Cibolo, a community 11 miles south of here, Saturday for the purpose of celebrating the 100 birthday of her father, Robert Schaefer. He was born on the 22nd day of August 1831. He has lived the greater part of his life in the near vicinity. Enjoying the unusual occasion with him were his son, Hugo Schaefer, of New Braunfels, Mrs. Antonia Keudell of Cibolo, and Mrs. Emma Schuwirth of Converse.

Sources

FORGOTTEN ROADS AND TEXAS TRAVELERS

1850 Census Bexar County, Texas
1850 Census Guadalupe County, Texas
1850 Census, Travis County, Texas
1860 Census, Comal County, Texas
1870 Census, Comal County, Texas
1880 Census, Bexar County, Texas
A History of Guadalupe County, Willie Mae Weiman
"A Stagecoach Named Houston," Mike Cox, Teas escapes.com
Alamo Studies Forum
Annals of Travis County and the City of Austin, Vol 61850
Austin-American, August 15, 1915
Baker, T. Lindsay, Gangster Tour of Texas
Battles and Men of the Republic of Texas, Arthur Wylie
Bexar County Deeds, 1850
Camino Del Norte: How a Series of Watering Holes and Fords and Dirt Trails Became a Highway, Horace Erchman
Celerity and Mud Wagons, True World, April 10, 2017, Marshall Trimble
Cibolo Centennial Cook Book and Reflections on the Last 100 Years 1876-1976

Clark, John Jr., Robbins, Elizabeth, McAron, A. Joachim, A Texas Legacy, the Old San Antonio Road and the Caminos Reales

Dallas Daily Herald, January 3, 1881

De Golyer Library, Southern Methodist University

Democratic Telegraph and Texas Register, Vol 11, No. 18, May 6, 1846

Ettiger, Josephine, Sweetest You Can Find

Family Footsteps, Vol VII, No. 3, 1990

Galveston Daily News, Vol 42, April 22, 1883

Galveston Weekly News, Vol 8, No. 23, July 8, 1851

Getting the Lay of the Land, Pioneer Surveying in Texas

Goff, Myra Lee Adam, The Sophienburg, "Mensebach personal despite pestilence, poverty"

Gretchen, Mark, Slave Transactions of Guadalupe County, Texas

Guadalupe County Court Minutes, 1886-1896

Guadalupe Gazette, October 20, 1930 Jean Heide, The Stagecoach Line

Houston, A History and Guide, American Guide Series, Writers Program of the Work Project Administration

Houston Telegram / Texas Register, November 5, 1845

Houston Telegraph and Texas Register, October 28, 1838

http://www.txgenweb2.org/tx/guadalupe/guadalupe.txt

Index to Military Rolls of the Republic of Texas, 1835-1845

Indian Affairs Laws and Treaties, Vol 3

Johnson, Frank White, *A History of Texas and Texans*, Volume 4

Leon Springs Elementary, 1886-1989 History

Letter from Bishop of San Antonio, 1852

Letter from W.E. Jones to Governor E.M Pearce, September 24, 1855

Lich, Glen, The Germans in Texas

Lone Star and Southern Watch Tower, Vol 2, July 5, 1851

Lone Star and Southern Watch Tower, Vol 2, No. 21, July 12, 1851

Long, S.A., The Texas Stock Directory, Book of Marks, and Brands

Lost Texas Roads

Martinillo, Maria, The Search for Pedro's Story

Morgenthaler, Jefferson, *German Settlement of the Texas Hill Country*

O. Henry, *The Complete Works of O. Henry*

Our Heritage, Winter 1992-93, Vol 34, No. 2, San Antonio Genealogical Society

Race and Slavery Petitions Project, University of North Carolina, Digital Library on American Slaves.

"Rough and Ready in Illinois," Illinois Heritage, Vance Martin, and Mark SorensSpellman, Paul, Captain John R. Rogers, Texas Ranger

"Rough Riders," *Texas Monthly*, March 2016, Lou Taylor

Sam Houston's Texas, Sun Flanagan

San Antonio Conservation Society Journal, Vol 41, No. 3, Summer, 2005, Linda Persy and Jean Heide*San Antonio Daily Express*, October 23, 1905

San Antonio Express News, January 22, 2012

San Antonio Ledger, Vol 2, No. 1, May 28, 1857

San Antonio Stage Lines, 1847-1881, Robert Thonhoff

San Antonio Transportation Museum, Hugh Hemphill

San Marcos Free Press, Vol X, October 20, 1881

Sansom, John and Williams, R.W., *Massacre on the*

Nueces
Savage Frontier, Vol II, 1830-1835, Stephen L. Moore
Seele, Hermann. *The Cypress and Other Writings of a Texas Pioneer*
Slave Schedules, United States
"Stagecoach Service in the 1860's," Desert USA, Jay Sharp
Stagecoaches and Mud Wagons, Smithsonian Postal Museum
Stagecoaching in Texas, Texas Almanac, Mike Cox
Stirpes, Vol 6, No. 2, June 1866
Telegraph and Texas Register, Vol 10, No. 8, February 19, 1845
Telegraph and Texas Register, Vol 16, No. 20, May 18, 1851
Telegraph and Texas Register, Vol 16, August 23, 1851
Telephone and Texas Register, Vol 10, No. 52, December 31, 1845
Texas Democrat, Vol 2, No. II, March 20, 1847
Texas Presbyterian, Vol, No. 1, November 13, 1846
Texas Presbyterian, Vol 1, No. 1, January 2, 1847
Texas Presbyterian, Vol, No. I, February 13, 1847
Texas State Gazette, Vol 1, No. 22, January 19, 1850
Texas State Gazette, Vol 2, No. 35, April 19, 1851
Texas State Gazette, Vol 3, November 1851
Texas State Gazette, March 22, 1852
Texas State Gazette, Vol 3, No. 46, July 3, 1852
Texas State Times, Vol 2, No. 37, August 8, 1855
Texas Stock Directory, 1865
Texas Supreme Court, 3 Texas 7, 1848, Tarbox vs. Kennon
Texas Supreme Court, Reports of Cases argued and

decided in the Supreme Court of Texas, Volume 16
Texian Advocate, Vol 3, No. 44, March 21, 1849
The Colorado Herald, Vol 2, Ed. 1, January 15, 1847
The Harrison-McCulloch Stage Stop, 1850-1854, Jean Heide
The Indian Papers of Texas, Dorman H. Winfery and James Day editors
The Laws of Texas, 1822-1897, Volume 3
The New York Herald, May 10, 1849
The Personal Correspondence of Sam Houston, 1839-1845, Sam Houston
The Stagecoach, *Tombstone Times*
The Statutes at Large and Treaties of the United States, Vol 9
The Story of William Walker and His Associates, William O. Scroggs
The Texas Report: Cases Adjudged in the Supreme Court, Vol 23
The U.S. Army on the Texas Frontier, 1845-1900, Thomas T. Smith
Transcribers Guild
Travelers in Texas, 1761-1860, Marjorie Sibley. *Seguin Enterprise*, 1924Texan by Teran, edited by John Wheaton
Travis County Deeds, E:258
Travis County Deeds, Reverse Index, 1842-1893, E-K
Travis County Deeds, Reverse Index, 1842-1893, S-Z
Turning Adversity into Advantage: A History of the Lipan Apaches of Texas and New Mexico, Nancy M. Minor
Usgwarchives.org/tx/Guadalupe/bios
Voyage to America, Prince Carl of Solms' Texas Diary
Weekly Democratic Statesman, Vol 12, No. 58, April 16,

1883
With Walker in Nicaragua, James C. Jones

SOURCES FOR THE GRANGE ON MAIN STREET

Bender, James, "History of the Original Texas State Grange," Southwestern Historical Quarterly, April 1939, Vol. XLII

Cibolo Grange Scrapbooks, 1952-1999

The Gilder Lehrma, Institute of American History

The San Antonio Express News, 1941-1999

The Seguin Herald, 1941-1999

Womack, Judy, Cibolo, Texas The Early Years Guadalupe County

SOURCES FOR WORLD WAR I

1850 Guadalupe County, Texas

1860 Guadalupe County, Texas

1870 Guadalupe County, Texas

1880 Travis County, Texas

Campbell, Randolph, *The Laws of Slavery in Texas*

Dick, Everett, *The Dixie Frontier: A Social History of the Southern Frontier*

Draft, Selective Service Roll, National Archives

Frantz, Joe. *Texas, A History*

Gesick, John Jr. *Under the Live Oak Tree*

Gretchen, Mark, Slave Transactions of Guadalupe County, Texas

Guadalupe County Commissioners Court Minutes, 1849-1862

Guadalupe County District Court, 1854-1855

Guadalupe County Tax Schedules, 1850-1860

Harter, J. Morris, *Trail Drives of Texas*

Honorable Treachery: A History of U.S. Intelligence and Espionage
Hough, Emerson, *The Web*
McDonald, Jason, Racial Dynamics in Early Twentieth Century Austin, Texas
McIntyre, Jennifer, M.A. Thesis, Texas Tech, Allegiance and Heritage: The German Americans of Fredericksburg, Texas in the Nazi Era
Seguin Enterprise, November 16, 1918
The Enemy Within—1994 television movie remake of 1964 film "Seven Days in May"Tucker, Spencer, Encyclopedia of World War I

SOURCES FOR THOMAS J. PERRYMAN

Bender, James, History of the Original Texas State Grange
German American Annals, Vol. 7
Report of Cases in Law and Equity, Georgia Supreme Court
San Antonio Ledger, Vol. 5, August 1855
Southwestern Historical Quarterly, April 1939, Vol. 17
Spellman, Paul. *Captain John H. Rogers, Texas Ranger*
Womack, Judy, Cibolo, Texas Guadalupe County, The Early Years
Texas State Gazette, October 1854
The Institute of American History, The Gilder Lehman
The Seguin Herald, 1855

Photo credits:
Jim Burdett, Sandra Lee Cleary, Bonnie George, Sabrina McKaskle Glazener, Cassandra Kearns, Mrs. George Sassmann

INDEX

Adams, Henry -129
Adelsverein –5,6,7
Ahr, Mr. -123
Amacher, Melchior -18, 111, 123
Alarcon's expedition -2, 52
Anderson, W.W. -16, 27, 111
Anthony, Abraham -18
      Beverly -119
Austin, Moses -2
      Stephen F. -2, 53, 54
Baeyer, Bernard -115
      Melchior -115
Banishment Act -109
Barrientes, Carmillo -119
Battle of Salado Creek -5
Baxter, William C. -9
Benning, Dr. H -124
Bergfeld, J.G. -20
Bertier. Charles -17
Biesenbach, Wallace -172
Biser, Carl -144
Blumberg, August -128,137
Blume, G. -125
      Max -125
Boerne State Bank -171
Bolton, Olivia -124
Bracht, Dr. Felix -15, 115
      Felicitas -16

Bracken - 95, 119, 167, 168
Bracken, William -10, 11
Brotz, Dorothy - 16
    Fred - 114
    Otto - 114, 117, 118, 128, 135
    Theresa - 129
Brown, John B. - 57 thru 101
Burbank, James - 17, 27, 111
Burdett, Jim - 138, 216
Caddo - 1, 49
Cadena, Jose Maria - 9, 10
Caldwell, Col. Matthew - 5
Camp Bowie - 147
Camp Clark - 113
Camp Swift - 181, 184
Camp Travis - 147, 163, 166, 167, 168
Carl, Prince of Solms-Braunfels - 6
Carlshaven - 6, 7
Castillo, Antonio - 119
C&E Grocery - 138
Certina, Michael - 119
Chisholm Trail - 38, 48
Cibolo Bank - 134, 151, 154
Cibolo City Park - 144
Cibolo Grain Company - 141
Cibolo Lumber Company - 137
Cibolo Mercantile - 141
Cibolo Valley - 1, 4, 25, 26, 45, 82, 118, 123, 128
Cibolo Volunteer Fire Department - 142
Coahiltecan - 1, 49, 50-60, 93
Comanche - 8, 49, 50, 51, 60, 94
Conrad, Carl - 16, 114
    Herman - 16
Conscription Act - 110

Contreres, Joseph - 119
    Michael - 119
Converse - 118, 177, 219
Coy, Emanuela De Los Santos - 9
Crescent Bend Dance Hall - 172
Crockett, Davy - 2, 4, 55
Crueger, Charles - 17
Curtis, Isaac - 119
Cut Off - 118
Dabney, William - 16
De Castro, Chief Duelgas - 9, 50
de Cordova, Jacob - 127
De La Garza, Frailen - 9, 11
De los Rios, Domingo - 2
Dewitt, Green - 11, 53
Diaz, Pablo - 112
Dietz, Edward - 126
    Ferdinand - 12, 17, 115, 226
    Gottlieb - 115
    Robert - 138
Doane, Jesse - 143
Doerr, Adaline - 138
Dominguez, Sexto - 9
Duff, Captain James - 112
Dykes, Ted - 144
Eason, William - 139
East, Henry - 123
El Camino Real de las Tejas - 2
Enseria, Joseph - 119
Fields, Henry - 18
Fisher, John - 124
Flacco, Chief - 50
Fling, Charles - 143, 182, 184, 186, 194
Fortune, Francis - 18

Forty Eighters - 15
Fromme, Alwinne - 129
    Carl - 115, 133, 142
    Charles - 120
Fromme's Gin - 119, 136
Galveston, Harrisburg, and San Antonio Railway - 117, 118
Garcia, Jesus - 18
Garcia, Trinidad - 9, 10
Gerhard, George - 17
Graves, Moses - 18
Gray, James - 9, 11
Griggs, Sam - 119
Grobe, August - 138
    Henry - 114
    Otto - 138
Grooms, M.O. - 144
Guadalupe Gazette - 147, 163
Haecker, Alwin - 134
    John - 127
Harboth, Emil - 137, 138
Harmon, Silas - 9
Hays, William - 134
Hayes, Texas Ranger Jack Hayes Coffee - 50
Heger, Charles - 17
    Fred - 17
Henderson, George - 18
Higgins, Joseph - 18
Hicks, John - 131, 135
Hild, Charley - 115
    Edward - 124
    George - 17
Hoffman, Henry - 17
Houston, General Sam - 4, 5, 6, 59, 73, 83, 109
Jackson, George - 18

Jacobson, Dr. Hilmer - 15, 16
Jansen, A.G. - 134
Jennull, Ernest - 19
Johnson, John - 119
Johnston, W.B. - 17, 111
Karankawa - 1
Keuler, Velaska - 139
Kiefer, Charles - 134
Kierum, Marvin - 143
Kniber, John - 17
Kopplin, Ernest - 172
LaVernia - 57, 131
Las Huerto del Mindo - 4
Latimer, Ben - 18
Leal, Jacob - 11
Lieck, Alwin - 143, 144, 178
Lindenburg, Matthias - 11
Ling, Linda - 143, 144
Lipan - 1, 8, 49, 50, 93
Lockhart, Byrd - 52, 54, 57
Los Corralitas - 3
Lower Valley - 16, 113, 120, 122, 152
Marion - 176, 177, 191, 192, 202 - 212
McKinley, William - 131
Meek, Tommy - 135, 143, 178
Meiners, Otto - 120
Meurin, T.P. - 17
Meyer, Edward - 134, 136
      Johanna - 135
Micheli, Vicenti - 11
Miller, David - 10
Mission San Antonio de Valero - 3
Mission San Juan Bautista - 1
Monte Galvan Ranch - 3

Murphy, John - 177, 179
    Pearl - 135
National Grange - 176, 188, 193, 201, 204, 208, 210
Neptune - 8
New Berlin - 12
New Braunfels - 2, 7, 13, 19, 40-45, 65-68, 72, 77, 80, 117, 140, 158, 161, 169, 204, 217, 219
New Braunfels State Bank - 171
New Braunfels Woolen Manufacturing Company (NBWMC) - 39, 40
Neu-Braunfelser Zeitung - 12
Newton Boys Gang - 171
Niemetz, Fred - 144
Oekin, Henry - 17
Orr, Henry - 17
Pearl's Bar - 135
Perryman, Elizabeth - 27, 28, 29, 34, 41
    Harmon - 21
    Thomas - 14, 16, 21-30, 33, 38, 40, 45, 48, 80, 82, 85, 111
    Thomas (T.J.) - 16, 27, 28, 36, 41, 47
Peters, Moses - 119
    Ottom - 125
    Will - 125
Pfannstiel, J. P. - 17, 111
Pfeil, Anton - 124, 134, 178
    Alfred - 141
    Edmund - 117
    Ewald - 137, 138, 172, 179
    Jacob - 123
    Maria - 118
    R.A. - 124
    Richard - 129
Podeval, Theodore - 114
Preston, Prekill - 18

Pumper team - 143
Rabe, Henry - 128
Raggedy - 146
Rainey, Joseph - 119
Rancho de San Francisco - 4, 11
Rancho Gortavi - 3
Rancho Leal - 3
Randolph Air Field Storm - 141
Rawe, Emil - 136, 143
Red Ball - 139
Red and White Grocery - 139
Reinhold, James - 17
Richardson, James - 9
Rinehart, Frank - 17
Rittiman, John - 17
Robinson, James - 18
Roosevelt, Teddy - 130
Rudy's - 135
Sahr, Alfred - 124
Samuel, Rev. Oscar - 20, 123
San Antonio Stats Freitung - 12
San Miguel de Amoladeras - 3
San Miguel, Pedro - 9
Santa Anna - 4, 5, 54, 55
Santa Clara - 13, 27, 34, 120
Sassman, George - 183, 184
Sassmanhausen, Louis - 115
Schaefer, Agnes - 133
    Hugo - 133, 219
    Robert - 133, 219
Schertz, Eugene - 171
Schlather, Anna - 20
    Ernst - 124, 139, 141. 178, 180
Schmitz, August - 120, 122

Schnabel, O.P. - 134
Schraub, A. G. - 134, 135
    Alfred - 177
    Arthur - 134
    Jacob - 132
    Oscar - 135
    Philip - 114
    Sophia - 16
Schuel, Adolph - 171
Schul, Babienda - 139
Scull, W.T. - 8, 9
Seiler, William - 17, 111
Shimmelpfenning, August - 114
Smidley, John - 18
Smith, Milton - 18
Sneed, Harrison - 18, 119, 141
Square Heads - 146
Stachelhausen, Ludwig - 132
Stapper, Edward - 16, 172, 179
    Gertrude - 20
    Hilmar - 178
    Joseph - 127
    T.L. - 17
St. Paul's Church - 139
Tarbox, Lyman - 57 thru 108
Taylor, Jack - 18
Tewes, Edwin - 12
Texas in the Year 1848 - 15
Thomas, Eliot - 18
Thomas, Kilfer - 18
Tipps, C.E - 134
Tory, Julian - 18
Tonkawa - 1, 49, 51, 52, 60, 94
Trotti, Carl - 144

D.O - 144
Vera - 139
Tschoepe, Eugene - 177, 179
Turknett - 112
Uhr, Henry - 124, 134, 135
Umphreys, Jim - 9
Union Loyal League - 112
Voight, Rudy - 135
Vordenbaum, Edgar - 143
    Frederick - 12
    Louis - 127
    Maria - 132
    Robert - 134
    R.W. - 124
    Sidney - 135
Weidner, Heinrich - 115
    Henrietta - 132
    Henry - 132
Weir, James - 31
Weller, Anna - 20
    Gottfried - 20
Werner, Albert - 128, 137
    Fritz - 128, 131
Weyel, Adolph - 115
Wiederstein, Alwin - 137
    E.C. - 143
    O.G. - 138
West, Hugo - 134
Wichita - 1, 49
Yehl, Fred - 17, 111
    William -17
Zenner - 124

www.ingramcontent.com/pod-product-compliance
Lightning Source LLC
Chambersburg PA
CBHW030108100526
44591CB00009B/325